AF413829

THE LONG GAME

THE LONG GAME

DESIGNING A LIFE THAT COMPOUNDS

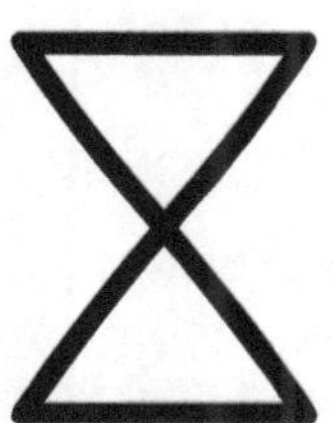

DANIEL GRIFFING

Long Game Press, Boston

Copyright © 2026 by Daniel Griffing

All rights reserved.

No part of this book may be reproduced, stored in a retrieval system, or transmitted in any form or by any means—electronic, mechanical, photocopying, recording, or otherwise—without the prior written permission of the publisher, except for brief quotations used in reviews or scholarly works.

Published by Long Game Press
Boston, Massachusetts

Hardcover ISBN: 979-8-9943516-0-4
Paperback ISBN: 979-8-9943516-1-1
Ebook ISBN: 979-8-9943516-2-8

Library of Congress Control Number: 2026910230
Printed in the United States of America

First edition

10 9 8 7   6 5 4 3 2 1

This book is for informational and educational purposes only. It does not constitute financial, medical, or legal advice. Readers should consult appropriate professionals before making decisions based on the content of this book.

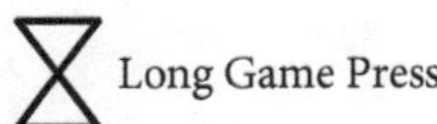

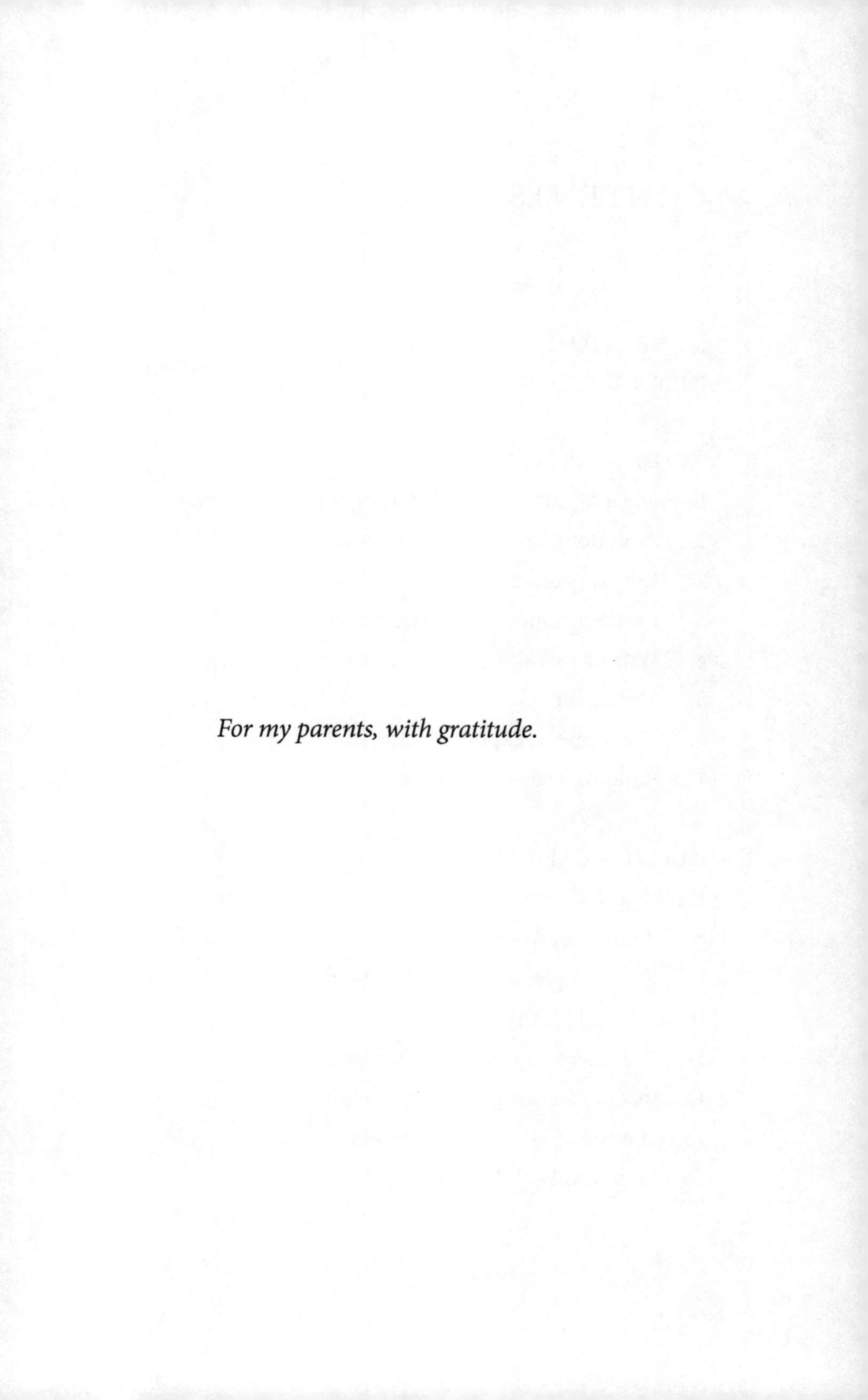

For my parents, with gratitude.

CONTENTS

MANIFESTO

This book begins with a simple belief—a good life is built, not optimized. It compounds across decades through attention, discipline, and care.

Intellect sharpens when curiosity is sustained. Capital grows when stewardship replaces urgency. Vitality endures when the body is treated as an asset rather than an afterthought. None of these domains stand alone. Each reinforces the others.

Alignment compounds. Drift compounds faster. Design your life so intellect, capital, and vitality reinforce one another.

Time is the constraint that gives this reinforcement meaning, and orientation determines whether it becomes an ally or an adversary. The long game is not about speed, perfection, or performance. It is about designing a life that holds—one that grows clearer, stronger, and more resilient with age.

What follows is an exploration of that design, not as a formula, but as a way of thinking for anyone committed to building a life that compounds.

INTRODUCTION
A Life Designed to Compound

There was a winter morning in Boston when I understood, with unusual clarity, that a life can be full yet narrow without our noticing. I had taken my usual seat in a small café near the waterfront, the kind of place where the city feels quiet for a few minutes before the day gathers its pace. I opened a worn Moleskine notebook I had carried during years of travel between Boston and London. I did it out of habit, not intention. The pages held notes I had written on early flights and late nights, during seasons of momentum and seasons of uncertainty. As I read through them, I felt a quiet dissonance between momentum and meaning.

Most people move through life without ever pausing to ask a simple question: *What, exactly, does it mean to live well for decades?* We are surrounded by advice on productivity, money, health, longevity, habits, routines, and purpose. Yet very little of it helps us understand how these pieces work together across a long life. We accumulate information, but not wisdom. We chase improvement, but we rarely design our lives with intention.

This book was born from the realization that a good life is not built in separate domains. It is built at the intersection of **intellect**, **capital**, and **vitality**. These three forces shape everything that matters, and they shape each other. Your mind influences your wealth, your wealth influences your health, your health influences your clarity, and your clarity influences every choice you make. Gradually, I realized these choices form a pattern. And the pattern becomes your life.

For years, I lived as many people do: focused on achievement, driven by responsibility, and carried forward by the momentum of a demanding career. I moved through countries and roles, led teams across borders, and checked every box a modern professional life places in front of you. The pace was constant. The progress was real. Yet somewhere along the way, I began to sense something important slipping beneath the surface. It was not energy or ambition that was fading. It was something quieter. It was the ability to think clearly and choose deliberately.

In my fifties, I began making changes that were small at first, yet significant in their cumulative effect. I simplified my environment, deepened my physical training, clarified my financial philosophy, refined what I read, and rebuilt my internal compass. I traveled more intentionally, wrote more consistently, and created space for reflection that had long been crowded out by efficiency. Eventually, I realized that these changes were not isolated improvements. They formed a system. And once the system emerged, my entire life began to compound.

I wrote this book for two groups of people. The first is those in their twenties and early thirties who want to build a life that compounds but are inundated with noise and unsure where to begin. The second is those in their forties, fifties, and beyond who feel the pull toward reinvention and want to design the next chapter with more clarity, depth, and intention. The principles in this book apply to both, because the long game is age-agnostic. Compounding works whether you begin early or begin now.

The structure of the book reflects this. **Part I, Intellect** explores how to build a mind that grows stronger across decades. It examines attention, curiosity, reading, writing, and the mental models that govern decision-making. **Part II, Capital** addresses money not as a symbol or scorecard, but as a source of freedom. It covers simplicity, investing, income design, tax strategy, and the philosophy of stewardship. **Part III, Vitality** focuses on the body as the chassis for everything else: strength, endurance, sleep, nutrition, mobility, and the pursuit of a long, powerful life.

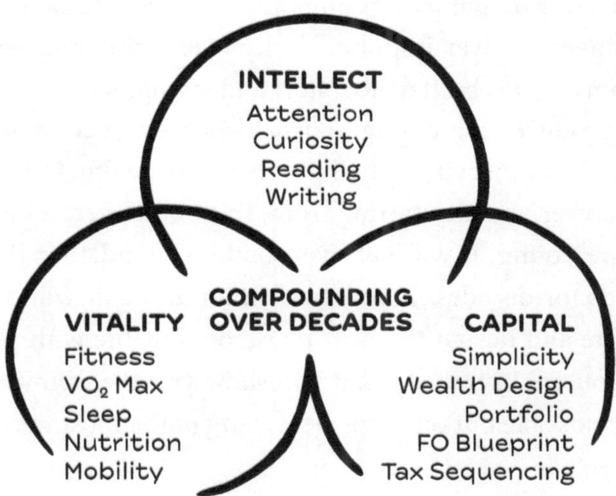

FIGURE 1 The Three Engines of a Long Life
Intellect, Capital, and Vitality compound together over decades. Each matters on its own, but it's their overlap, the space where attention, resources, and physical capacity align, that creates a life that grows richer, stronger, and more intentional with time.

I first sketched this framework years ago in a notebook, long before it became the organizing structure of this book. At the time, it was simply a way to make sense of the forces shaping my own life. Only later did I realize it was an architecture. And like any architecture, its strength depends on how its parts support one another.

Together, they form a single structure. Strength in one amplifies the others. Weakness in one eventually pulls the others down. When all three align, the trajectory of your life changes. You think more clearly, act more deliberately, and move with a sense of grounded momentum that is rare in the modern world.

Intellect sharpens judgment. Judgment improves capital allocation. Capital creates optionality. Optionality protects vitality. Vitality preserves capacity. And preserved capacity sustains intellect.

This is the long game. It is not a program, a hack, or a shortcut. It is a way of living that compounds. It rewards patience over speed, intention over impulse, clarity over noise, and resilience over intensity. It is built deliberately and strengthened daily. Over time, it produces something unusual—not just success, but freedom. Not just longevity, but vitality. Not just wealth, but wisdom.

Wherever you are starting from, this book offers a blueprint. If you are young, it will help you build a foundation that pays dividends for decades. If you are further along, it will help you recalibrate and design the next phase of your life with purpose. And if you are in transition, it will show you that reinvention is not only possible but often the beginning of the most meaningful chapter yet.

The long game is not about living forever. It is about living deliberately. It is about building a life that gets better, stronger, clearer, and deeper with time. It is the pursuit of a life well designed and well lived.

Let's begin.

PART I

INTELLECT

*Building a Mind That Grows
Stronger Across Decades*

CHAPTER 1
Attention: The First Principle

What you attend to shapes what you notice, what you value, and ultimately who you become.

decade ago, I was sitting in a café near Bellevueplatz in Zurich. Morning light rested on the surface of the lake, and the city was only beginning to stir. I remember the warmth of the coffee cup in my hands, the quiet of the early trams, and the sense of being briefly untouched by the demands of the day. That kind of stillness had become rare.

At the time, I was leading cross-border teams, and my mornings felt global before the sun was fully up. Messages waited, decisions piled up, and calendars seemed to fill on their own. It was the usual rhythm of my life. Yet on that morning, something broke through the pattern. As I worked through a familiar email, I realized I could not remember the last time I had experienced a clear, uninterrupted thought. The work still mattered, but my mind had not been still long enough for clarity to find me.

I looked up from my laptop and watched the trams pass through Bellevueplatz. In that ordinary moment, a truth surfaced. My attention was no longer mine. It had been slowly claimed by urgency masquerading as importance. That realization, simple as it was, marked the beginning of a deeper understanding. Attention, more than time or ambition, was the asset I had neglected most.

We talk often about goals, plans, careers, habits, and achievements. Yet all these sit downstream from a single upstream force: attention. What you attend to shapes what you notice, value, and pursue, and eventually who you become. Fragmented attention creates a fragmented life. This applies to every stage. In your twenties, attention determines which opportunities you even see. In midlife, it determines which paths you continue and which you finally abandon. No other human capacity compounds as invisibly or as powerfully.

The danger of fragmented attention is not that it makes you ineffective in any obvious way. Most people remain productive.

They meet deadlines, respond to messages, and advance in their careers. From the outside, nothing appears broken. The cost is quieter and more insidious. Fragmented attention erodes judgment long before it affects output.

I recognized this one afternoon after catching myself switching between email, news, and messages without finishing a single task. I closed my laptop and deleted two apps from my phone. It was not dramatic. No announcement. No vow. I simply removed the inputs that were pulling at me most often. The next morning felt unusually quiet. I noticed how much of my distraction had not been imposed from the outside, but invited.

When attention is divided, decisions become reactive rather than deliberate. You respond to what is loud rather than what is important. You optimize for immediacy over direction. This creates a life that feels busy but unmoored. Progress continues, but clarity diminishes. You move faster while becoming less certain about where you are going.

Long-term thinking pulls in the opposite direction. It requires delayed gratification, second- and third-order awareness, and a bias toward investments of time, attention, and capital that compound across years rather than quarters. It demands the ability to ignore what is urgent in order to protect what is enduring.

This is why distraction is so difficult to diagnose in ourselves. We associate failure with collapse, not with drift. Yet most lives do not derail suddenly. They drift gradually, carried by momentum rather than intention. Attention, when left unmanaged, becomes the steering mechanism that no longer answers to you. It responds instead to urgency, expectation, and habit.

The modern environment accelerates this process. Digital communication rewards speed and availability. Professional cultures equate responsiveness with competence. Social systems train us to treat interruption as normal and depth as indulgent. Gradually, we internalize these norms. We begin to feel uneasy in stillness. Silence becomes something to fill. Uninterrupted time feels unproductive, even when it is the source of our best thinking.

The long-term consequence is not simply fatigue. It is a narrowing of perspective. When attention is constantly pulled outward, reflection suffers. Curiosity weakens. You lose contact with the slower forms of understanding that require sustained presence. Important questions remain unasked, not because they are difficult, but because they require a quality of attention that has been crowded out.

This erosion compounds. Small decisions made without clarity accumulate. Opportunities aligned with your deeper interests go unnoticed. Commitments taken on reflexively become obligations that are difficult to unwind. Years later, you may find yourself successful by conventional measures yet uncertain how you arrived where you are. The issue was never effort. It was attention deployed without intention.

If I could sit across from my twenty-three-year-old self, eager and impatient to advance, I would offer one piece of guidance: protect your attention. What you allow into your mind becomes the scaffolding of your future. In youth, distraction feels harmless. You believe you can outwork it. You mistake motion for progress. The cost, however, arrives gradually.

By your fifties, you begin to feel that cost. Attention has been stretched and fractured in ways you never anticipated. Careers grow, responsibilities multiply, and digital communication expands. Expectations rise. Decisions accumulate. Cognitive and emotional bandwidth are taxed by countless small demands. You can spend years competent, productive, even admired, yet remain distant from your own thinking.

For many, this becomes permanent. For others, it becomes a turning point. My own fifties were the first time I began deliberately reclaiming my mind. Life had not become simpler. I had simply noticed the clarity I had traded away. The path back required removing more than adding: less noise, fewer inputs, more intentional days, longer walks, better reading, steady writing, and a measure of quiet that had been missing. Slowly, attention returned, bringing clarity with it.

One of the most persistent misconceptions is that attention is a matter of discipline. Research suggests otherwise. Roy Baumeister showed that willpower is easily depleted.[1] BJ Fogg demonstrated that environment shapes behavior more reliably than intention.[2] Cal Newport's work reveals that deep focus emerges from removing noise rather than forcing concentration.[3] What looks like discipline is usually design. Environments built for depth produce depth. Environments built for distraction produce distraction. This truth applies to every age and every ambition.

When you protect your attention, the returns are disproportionate. One uninterrupted hour of focus becomes more valuable than ten scattered hours of effort. A quiet walk can yield clarity that meetings never do. One carefully chosen book can redirect a decade. A year of intentional attention can unwind years of accumulated noise. Attention compounds like capital. Distraction accumulates like debt.

If attention is a form of capital, it deserves thoughtful allocation. Most people invest it unintentionally: too much lost to noise, too much consumed by obligation, too much diluted by low-quality distraction, and very little reserved for genuine growth. This pattern leads predictably to stagnation. A more deliberate allocation recognizes the primacy of focus, the value of high-quality inputs, the importance of curiosity, and the necessity of allowing space for life's natural imperfections. Perfection is unnecessary. Awareness is enough.

A simple question reveals more about your direction than almost anything else: Who currently owns my attention? Your answer explains your sense of clarity or confusion, your momentum or drift, your fulfillment or frustration. Attention is the foundation upon which every other part of life rests.

In the end, a long life well lived is the cumulative result of chosen inputs. What you read, who you listen to, what you focus on, what you release, and what you nourish. These choices shape identity, and identity shapes destiny. This is why we begin here, before capital and vitality. Attention is the first principle of the long game. Protect it. Cultivate it. Honor it. Everything else follows.

CHAPTER 2
Curiosity as a Strategy

*Curiosity keeps the future
larger than the past.*

There are seasons in life when curiosity comes naturally. In childhood, it is effortless. In adolescence, it is instinctive. Even in our early twenties, curiosity still carries us forward, guiding us toward people, places, and ideas that shape who we are becoming. But something happens as life grows more structured. Careers begin, responsibilities accumulate, routines solidify, and the world becomes narrower at the very moment when it should be expanding. Curiosity, once abundant, becomes something we must choose rather than something that appears.

For years, I believed curiosity was a personality trait. Some people had it and others did not. It took time and experience to understand that curiosity is not an accident. It is a practice. It is a way of moving through the world with attention, humility, and a willingness to be changed. It is both a mindset and a discipline, and its rewards compound in ways few people appreciate until much later in life.

The world rewards those who follow their curiosity more than those who follow a script. Yet most people abandon curiosity just when they need it most. Early in our careers there is pressure to be definitive. We want to appear knowledgeable, capable, and certain. Curiosity, by contrast, requires admitting what we do not know. It demands questions rather than answers. It asks us to suspend pride in favor of discovery. In environments that prize expertise, curiosity can feel uncomfortable. Yet without it, growth becomes impossible.

Curiosity is also one of the great antidotes to complacency. Many people begin living inside smaller circles of information and experience. Their assumptions harden. Their thinking narrows. They stop exploring because exploration does not feel productive. But growth and productivity are not the same thing. Curiosity brings renewal. It stretches the mind, and in stretching it, it keeps it alive.

There is also a practical side to curiosity that people underestimate. Curiosity improves decision-making. It exposes you to information you did not know you needed. It reduces blind spots. It encourages you to look at problems from more than one angle. When you are curious, you gather more data, consider more possibilities, and see patterns earlier. That becomes a strategic advantage.

In my own life, curiosity has often shown up as movement. From South Africa to Saudi Arabia to Vietnam, I have always felt a strong pull to explore new places, both geographically and intellectually. My travels across fifty countries were not attempts to escape my life. They were attempts to understand it. Each new place exposed me to different ways of thinking about work, family, health, ambition, and purpose. Curiosity broadened my worldview and anchored me at the same time. It gave me perspective, and perspective is one of the few things that cannot be taught directly. It must be lived.

Curiosity also shows up in quieter forms. It appears in the books we choose, the conversations we seek out, the questions we dare to ask, and the ideas we allow ourselves to entertain. Curiosity reveals itself in the willingness to read outside our comfort zone, to revisit beliefs we have held for years, and to admit that the world is always more complex than we once thought. In our twenties, this is natural. In our fifties, it becomes a discipline.

The danger of losing curiosity is not that life becomes immediately smaller. Most people remain competent, capable, and outwardly successful. They continue to perform well in familiar environments and make decisions that appear reasonable within the bounds of what they already know. The cost is quieter. When curiosity fades, learning slows long before performance does.

Without curiosity, the mind begins to close in on itself. Questions give way to conclusions. Exploration yields to explanation. This produces a subtle rigidity. You become efficient within a shrinking frame of reference. Decisions are made faster, but from a narrower base of information. What looks like confidence is often simply familiarity mistaken for understanding.

This is difficult to detect because certainty is rewarded. Professional environments favor decisiveness. Social settings often reward having an opinion more than holding an open question. As a result, curiosity can feel inefficient or even risky. Admitting uncertainty can appear weak. Asking questions can be misread as lack of expertise. Gradually, many people learn to suppress curiosity not because it lacks value, but because it carries social and professional friction.

The consequence is not ignorance, but blind spots. When curiosity recedes, assumptions harden. You stop testing your mental models against reality. You rely more heavily on past success to justify present decisions. This works for a time. Familiar strategies continue to deliver familiar results. But the world does not remain static. When conditions change, those who have not remained curious are the last to notice and the slowest to adapt.

Premature certainty also limits opportunity. Many of the most meaningful paths in life do not announce themselves clearly at the outset. They emerge gradually, through exposure, experimentation, and a willingness to follow questions before outcomes are obvious. Without curiosity, these paths remain invisible. You only see what fits your existing framework. Entire categories of possibility never register as options.

This narrowing becomes self-reinforcing. Reading becomes more selective. Conversations grow predictable. Experiences are filtered through what you already believe. The mind becomes organized but less flexible. Years later, you may find yourself accomplished yet restless, sensing that something is missing without being able to name it. The issue was not lack of ability or effort. It was the quiet abandonment of curiosity.

Curiosity, when practiced deliberately, prevents this outcome. It keeps judgment provisional. It creates space between stimulus and response. It allows you to revisit beliefs before they calcify into identity. Most importantly, it preserves adaptability. In a world that changes faster than any individual can predict, adaptability is not a soft trait. It is a strategic advantage.

A life designed to compound requires more than discipline and execution. It requires ongoing openness. Curiosity ensures that growth remains possible even when routines are established and success has already been achieved. The cost of abandoning it is not failure, but stagnation disguised as stability. Curiosity, sustained over decades, is what keeps a life expansive rather than merely efficient.

Reinvention begins with curiosity. You cannot build a better version of your life if you are not open to seeing your life differently. Curiosity is what allows this shift to take shape. It loosens the grip of old assumptions and introduces the possibility of change. It reminds us that growth is not limited to youth and that the most meaningful breakthroughs often occur when we are mature enough to appreciate them.

If attention determines your trajectory, curiosity determines your direction. Attention clears the space. Curiosity fills it. Together they form the starting point for any life that is designed to compound. Curiosity keeps the mind open, the spirit engaged, and the future larger than the past. It turns the world into a place of possibility rather than a place of routine.

To build a life that compounds, cultivate curiosity. Seek out new experiences even when your instincts tell you to stay comfortable. Read widely and deeply. Ask questions that challenge your assumptions. Travel not to escape, but to understand. Engage with people whose perspectives differ from your own. Allow yourself to follow interests that do not have an obvious outcome or immediate utility. These choices accumulate. They create a mind capable of sustained growth and a life that remains expansive rather than shrinking with age.

Curiosity is not an indulgence. It is a strategy. It is one of the few qualities that enhances every other part of life. It sharpens the intellect, enriches relationships, strengthens resilience, deepens creativity, and expands opportunity. Most importantly, it keeps you awake to your own potential.

Attention begins the work. Curiosity continues it. Together they form the foundation of the long game.

CHAPTER 3

Reading as an Asymmetric Advantage

*Reading is leverage
because its benefits compound.*

There are very few habits that produce outsized returns for such a small investment of time and attention. Reading is one of them. The world often treats reading as an academic exercise or a pastime, but in reality, it is one of the most powerful forms of leverage a person can cultivate. It enlarges your perspective, sharpens your thinking, expands your vocabulary of possibility, and introduces you to minds, eras, and ideas you would never encounter otherwise. Reading is not simply an activity. It is a way of widening your life.

When I look back over the last several decades, the periods of greatest clarity were often the periods when I was reading the most. This was no coincidence. When you read consistently, your thoughts become more structured, your decisions more grounded, and your understanding of the world more nuanced. Reading gives your mind new tools. It reveals patterns. It connects ideas that once seemed unrelated. Gradually, the mind begins to operate at a different depth.

Yet for many people, reading is something they stop prioritizing just when they need it most. In youth, time feels abundant and curiosity is natural. In midlife, time feels scarce, and reading becomes something people intend to return to "when things slow down," which they rarely do. The irony is that the busier and more responsible your life becomes, the more essential reading becomes. It is one of the few practices that restores clarity in a world that constantly fractures it.

Research supports what readers have known intuitively for centuries. Studies from Yale, Stanford, and the Max Planck Institute show that reading strengthens neural pathways, enhances memory, slows cognitive decline, and improves the brain's ability to process complex information. Research by psychologist Raymond Mar further suggests that reading fiction engages the cognitive systems we use to understand other people, shaping judgment, perspective, and emotional regulation across the lifespan.[4] Alan Jacobs observes in *The Pleasures of Reading* that sustained reading does more than sharpen cognition; it cultivates habits of attention and sympathy, gradually shaping the inner life from which judgment, imagination, and moral perception arise.[5]

I sometimes think about a late-night flight from Newark to Zurich that captured this truth in a single moment. The cabin lights had dimmed, most people were sleeping, and I opened a book I had packed without much thought. Somewhere over Europe, a single paragraph stopped me. It expressed something I had felt for years but had never articulated. I reread it several times, letting it settle. As the first light of morning appeared on the horizon and the plane began its descent into Switzerland, that small moment of clarity shifted how I understood a decision I had been postponing. Nothing dramatic happened, yet something inside me aligned. Books often do that. They change the angle from which you see your own life, sometimes in the span of a few quiet pages.

One of the quiet strengths of reading is that its effects accumulate. A single book rarely transforms you. Fifty books do. A decade of reading alters the architecture of your thinking in ways that become visible only in retrospect. The benefits appear slowly, then all at once. You begin to recognize patterns sooner, make decisions with more confidence, and hold your beliefs with more nuance. Wisdom is rarely loud, but it is unmistakable when it begins to accrue. Reading accelerates that process.

Reading also slows you down in a way that invites insight. The modern world rewards speed, immediacy, and constant reaction. Reading works in the opposite direction. It quiets the mind. It cultivates patience. It rewards full attention. It allows you to sit with another person's thoughts long enough for them to interact with your own. That simple act of slowing down often reveals clarity that constant motion conceals.

The danger of neglecting deep reading is not that you become uninformed. Most people remain well aware of current events, trends, and talking points. They consume headlines, podcasts, newsletters, and endless fragments of information throughout the day. From the outside, they appear knowledgeable. The cost is quieter and more consequential. Without sustained reading, thinking becomes thinner long before intelligence does.

Shallow inputs produce shallow integration. When information arrives in short bursts, the mind has little opportunity to wrestle with ideas long enough for them to take root. You collect facts without building frameworks. You recognize concepts without understanding their origins or limits. This creates the illusion of insight without its substance. Opinions form quickly but rest on fragile foundations.

This is difficult to notice because modern information systems reward speed and breadth. Being "up to date" is treated as a proxy for understanding. Yet depth rarely emerges from immediacy. It emerges from patience, context, and repetition. Books provide these conditions. They force the mind to stay with an idea long enough to encounter its complexity. Without that friction, thinking remains reactive, shaped more by exposure than by judgment.

When reading is replaced by summaries alone, another subtle shift occurs. You begin borrowing conclusions rather than developing them. Ideas arrive already packaged, stripped of the reasoning that produced them. This saves time, but it weakens discernment. You may know *what* to think without fully understanding *why*. This erodes intellectual independence. Your thinking becomes increasingly derivative, even when it feels confident.

The compounding effect of shallow inputs appears gradually. Conversations grow repetitive. New ideas feel familiar too quickly. You find yourself reaching for the same explanations in different contexts. The mind becomes efficient but less original. What once felt like curiosity begins to resemble consumption. Reading less does not leave a vacuum. It allows other, noisier inputs to take its place.

Deep reading resists this drift. It slows the pace of thought. It demands sustained attention and rewards it with structure. When you read a book carefully, you inhabit another person's reasoning. You follow an argument from its premises to its conclusions. You encounter uncertainty, contradiction, and revision. This process strengthens the mind's ability to hold complexity without rushing to resolution.

This changes how you think even when you are not reading. You become more patient with ambiguity. You ask better questions. You recognize patterns earlier because you have encountered them in different forms before. The benefits are not linear. They accumulate until they begin to shape judgment itself.

A life designed to compound requires more than access to information. It requires the capacity to integrate it. Reading deeply builds that capacity. Without it, the mind remains busy but underdeveloped, informed but unanchored. The issue was never a lack of intelligence or effort. It was reliance on inputs too shallow to support sustained insight.

Over the years, I have found that reading deepens even further when I take the time to synthesize what it gives me. I use a simple system in Notion to capture the ideas that resonate, the passages that challenge me, and the questions a book leaves behind. I do not treat it as homework. I treat it as a way of noticing what matters. These notes become a kind of intellectual trail, allowing ideas from different books to speak to one another. Often, I return to them months later and discover connections I did not see the first time. In this way, reading becomes not just consumption but reflection, and reflection is what allows insight to compound.

As we age, another benefit becomes clear: reading protects the mind from narrowing. Without intention, our intellectual world contracts. We return to familiar ideas, familiar opinions, familiar mental grooves. Reading pushes against that contraction. It introduces novelty, discomfort, and possibility. It keeps the mind open. Curiosity lives longer in people who read.

For someone in their twenties, reading offers early leverage that cannot be matched by any other habit. It accelerates wisdom at the beginning of life's curve. For someone in midlife, reading becomes a tool of reinvention. It reopens internal rooms that have been closed for years. It gives shape to reflection and perspective to decision-making. And for someone later in life, reading can offer companionship, meaning, and the ongoing experience of growth.

The long game rewards behaviors that compound. Reading is one of the purest examples of this. It strengthens your intellect, deepens your understanding of yourself and the world, and improves the quality of your inner life. It enriches your quiet moments and sharpens your active ones. It becomes the unseen structure beneath a better life.

If attention is the foundation and curiosity the spark, reading is the fuel. Together, they create a mind that expands rather than contracts with age. Reading does more than inform you. It shapes you. And in shaping you, it shapes the life you are capable of building.

CHAPTER 4
Writing to Think Clearly

Writing reveals what thinking conceals.

There comes a time when thought must give way to action. A moment when thinking alone is no longer enough, when ideas feel crowded, decisions circle without resolution, and clarity sits just out of reach. It is in these moments that writing becomes invaluable. Writing does something that thinking cannot accomplish on its own. It slows the mind down enough for it to reveal itself. It takes the abstract and makes it tangible. It converts confusion into structure. Writing is not merely a communication skill. It is a discipline of clarity.

I did not always understand this. Early in my career, writing was something I did because the job required it: emails, presentations, strategy documents, leadership updates. That writing was functional. It served its purpose. Eventually, I realized that the writing I did for myself—the quiet, private writing in notebooks, on long flights, or during early mornings before the world stirred—was far more powerful. Those pages created space for my thinking to breathe. They revealed what I truly believed and clarified what I wanted to do next. Writing allowed me to examine my own mind free of the pressure to impress or perform.

At some point in midlife, after making decisions at a relentless pace, I began relying on writing in a more intentional way. I wrote to understand what I was feeling. I wrote to separate signal from noise. I wrote to evaluate decisions, to reflect on choices, and to explore possibilities I had not yet named. Writing became not just a habit but a form of calibration. It steadied my internal world.

A tool that became surprisingly important in this process was my Moleskine notebook. I carry it almost everywhere. It is where I jot down early ideas, questions I want to revisit, frameworks that emerge in fragments, and insights that surface at unexpected moments. I do not treat it as a formal journal. I treat it as a landing place for thoughts that are not yet ready for structure. Some pages contain a single sentence. Others hold half-formed diagrams or phrases I want to explore later. It has become a steady companion to my thinking, a place where ideas form before I know what they will become.

The power of writing lies in its ability to externalize thought. When ideas stay in your mind, they feel cohesive. When you try to write them down, you discover their edges and their gaps. Writing exposes the difference between what you think you know and what you actually understand. This is why writing has been a foundational practice for thinkers throughout history. Seneca wrote letters to clarify his philosophy. Marie Curie kept meticulous scientific journals. Leonardo da Vinci filled notebooks with sketches, questions, and unfinished ideas as he worked to understand the world. The act of writing forces a kind of intellectual honesty that thinking alone cannot produce.

Most problems remain complicated until you force them into clarity. Thinking rarely does this. Writing does. I learned this years ago during a morning in London. I had woken early, long before the rest of the city, and sat in the hotel lounge with my notebook. I had been thinking about the next chapter of my life and could not tell if the path ahead was intentional or simply inherited momentum. I had circled the question without gaining traction. That morning, almost instinctively, I opened the Moleskine and began writing the problem as if I were explaining it to someone else. As the words formed, the issue reorganized itself on the page. What had felt complicated in my mind became unexpectedly simple in writing. Within fifteen minutes, the answer that had eluded me for weeks appeared, almost casually, in the margin. I closed the notebook and felt a quiet certainty settle in. Writing had done what thinking alone could not.

The danger of not writing is that your thinking doesn't

disappear—it blurs. Most people think constantly. Ideas circulate, decisions are rehearsed internally, and conversations replay long after they end. From the outside, nothing seems amiss. The cost is quieter. When thought remains internal, it often feels clearer than it truly is.

Unwritten ideas tend to retain the illusion of coherence. In the mind, contradictions blur together. Gaps go unnoticed. Ambiguity feels manageable because it has not yet been tested. Writing removes this protection. It forces thought into sequence. It demands that one idea follow another. In doing so, it exposes what is incomplete, inconsistent, or poorly understood. Without writing, many people mistake familiarity with clarity.

This is why unresolved decisions linger. When choices remain unarticulated, they feel complex and heavy. The mind circles them repeatedly without progress. Writing interrupts this loop. It creates distance between the thinker and the thought. Once an idea is on the page, it can be evaluated rather than rehearsed. Without that separation, thinking becomes recursive rather than constructive.

Modern life amplifies this problem. Speed is rewarded. Reaction is constant. There is little space for sustained reflection, and even less encouragement to slow thought down long enough to examine it. Many people substitute activity for clarity. They move forward while carrying unresolved assumptions, untested beliefs, and partially formed intentions. Writing, when absent, allows this accumulation to persist unnoticed.

Unexamined thought produces subtle drift. Decisions are made based on momentum rather than intention. Priorities blur. Values become implicit rather than chosen. You may remain productive, even successful, while feeling increasingly disconnected from the reasoning that guides your life. The issue is not lack of intelligence or experience. It is the absence of a process that forces thought into honesty.

Writing provides that process. It does not guarantee good decisions, but it makes poor reasoning harder to sustain. When you write, you confront your own logic. You see what you are avoiding. You notice patterns that repeat. This is uncomfortable at times, but it is also clarifying. Writing does not flatter the thinker. It reveals them.

The compounding effect of writing emerges slowly. A single page rarely changes much. But a habit of externalizing thought reshapes how you think even when you are not writing. You become more precise with language. More aware of assumptions. More deliberate in decision-making. Clarity ceases to be episodic. It becomes a baseline.

A life designed to compound requires more than insight. It requires integration. Writing is one of the few practices that reliably transforms insight into understanding. Without it, thought remains diffuse and impressionistic. With it, ideas acquire structure and weight. The issue was never a lack of thinking. It was thinking left unexamined.

Writing is also one of the most effective tools for identifying patterns in your own life. When you write regularly, themes begin to reappear: questions you keep asking, decisions you keep delaying, or values you keep returning to. These patterns matter. They reveal what you are wrestling with and what you are ready to grow into. Your writing becomes a map of your inner landscape. It shows you where you have been and points toward where you need to go next.

The benefits of writing extend beyond clarity. Writing deepens memory and learning. Psychologists call this the "generation effect," the finding that information is better encoded when you generate it rather than simply consume it. Writing is an act of generation. It forces your mind to engage, interpret, and create. When you write about an idea, you not only remember it more effectively, but you also understand it more deeply. This makes writing a natural complement to reading. Reading fills the mind. Writing organizes it.

My writing practice remains simple. I do not keep strict rules or complex systems. I use a combination of notebooks, digital files, and a clean structure in Notion where I refine the ideas that matter most. Some days the writing is only a few sentences. Other days it becomes a longer exploration. The goal is never to produce something polished. The goal is to think. Writing is the process that makes that possible.

One of the quiet truths about writing is that consistency matters more than intensity. Ten minutes a day is more valuable than two hours once a week. Writing rewards repetition. The more often you return to the page, the deeper and more honest your thinking becomes. Thoughts that once felt vague become clear. Decisions that felt heavy become manageable. Emotions that felt tangled begin to separate. Writing creates structure. It creates space.

For someone in their twenties, writing is a way to understand themselves during a period of rapid change. It clarifies values and reveals direction. For someone in midlife, writing becomes a tool of reorientation. It separates who you were from who you are becoming. And for someone later in life, writing can serve as a legacy, a companion, and a way to deepen the meaning of lived experience.

The long game is built on a foundation of clear thinking. Writing strengthens that foundation. It sharpens your mind, reveals what matters, and transforms internal noise into clarity. Writing does not require perfection. It requires presence. It requires the willingness to sit with your own mind long enough for it to organize itself.

If attention is the foundation, curiosity the spark, and reading the fuel, then writing is the structure that shapes them. It turns input into insight and insight into wisdom. Writing becomes a companion to your growth, steady, honest, and transformative.

In the end, writing is not about producing pages. It is about producing clarity. And clarity is one of the most powerful advantages you can cultivate over the course of a long life.

CHAPTER 5

Mental Models:
How to Think in Decades

*Mental models turn
experience into judgment.*

Progress doesn't hinge on how much you know, but on how clearly you think. Sooner or later, that truth becomes impossible to ignore. You begin to realize that the quality of your decisions matters far more than the quantity of your knowledge. You become more aware of the patterns that repeat, the mistakes that compound, and the opportunities that appear only when you are positioned to recognize them. This is where mental models become essential. Mental models are the lenses through which we interpret the world. They shape how we analyze problems, how we weigh risk, how we evaluate opportunities, and how we make decisions that reverberate across years or even decades.

I did not encounter the idea of mental models early in my life. Like many people, I spent my early career relying on instinct, effort, and experience. It was only later that I came across Charlie Munger's writing and speeches, and they changed the way I approached thinking itself. Munger believed that to make better decisions, you needed a latticework of models drawn from a wide range of disciplines: psychology, economics, biology, engineering, history, mathematics, and human behavior. His insight was simple and profound: The world is too complex to understand through a single lens. Clear thinking requires multiple lenses.

This resonated with me because I had already lived the experience of moving across different cultures, companies, and continents. Working in Switzerland taught me how Europeans approached strategy, collaboration, and patience. Working across the Middle East and Africa revealed different conceptions of risk, time, and resilience. Working between Boston and London showed me how two Western cultures could interpret the same data in very different ways. Without realizing it at the time, these experiences expanded my own mental models. Munger simply gave me the language for what I had already begun practicing.

Mental models do something important: They prevent you from being trapped in the assumptions of your current environment. They give you the ability to step back, shift your perspective, and reconsider a problem from a different angle. They help you recognize when you are overconfident, when you are missing something obvious, or when a situation resembles a pattern you have seen before. The world may change, but the underlying forces that drive human behavior change very slowly, if at all. Mental models help you see those forces at work.

One of the most useful lessons I drew from Munger was the value of thinking in decades rather than days. Most people anchor their decisions to short-term considerations: the next meeting, the next quarter, the next year. But life becomes clearer when you zoom out. When you think in decades, the noise falls away. Certain decisions suddenly reveal their true weight. Others lose their urgency. Thinking long-term allows you to differentiate between what is merely pressing and what is truly important.

This shift is not about predicting the future. It is about building a worldview that remains stable as the world moves around you. It is about cultivating a mind that can evaluate decisions in terms of trajectory, not immediate reward. It is about recognizing that compounding works in thinking just as it does in investing. Small advantages today can grow into large advantages. Small mistakes left unchecked can turn into large ones. Mental models help you recognize those early signals.

The danger of poor thinking is not that it produces obviously bad outcomes. Most people make decisions that are reasonable in the moment. They respond to incentives, manage near-term risks, and solve the problems directly in front of them. From the outside, their choices often look sensible. The cost is cumulative.

Without durable mental models, decisions stack without coherence, and progress stalls rather than collapsing outright.

Short-horizon thinking favors immediacy over trajectory. It optimizes for what is visible and measurable now, often at the expense of what compounds later. When decisions are evaluated in isolation, rather than as part of a longer arc, trade-offs are obscured. Small compromises seem harmless. Convenience replaces principle. These decisions shape a life that feels reactive rather than designed.

This pattern is difficult to recognize because the environment reinforces it. Modern systems reward speed, responsiveness, and quarterly results. Long-term thinking can feel abstract or impractical when immediate demands press constantly. As a result, many people confuse busyness with progress. They move decisively but without a framework that connects today's choices to tomorrow's outcomes.

Single-lens thinking compounds the problem. When problems are approached from only one discipline or perspective, blind spots multiply. Psychological incentives are ignored. Second-order effects are overlooked. Historical parallels go unrecognized. What appears rational within a narrow frame can be deeply flawed when viewed through a wider one. Mental models exist precisely to counter this tendency. They force perspective shifts that reveal what linear thinking conceals.

The absence of mental models also makes error correction harder. Without them, mistakes are often attributed to bad luck or external circumstances rather than flawed assumptions. Patterns repeat because they are never examined structurally. Decisions feel familiar even when outcomes disappoint. This erodes confidence and clarity, not because the individual lacks intelligence, but because their thinking lacks scaffolding.

Thinking in decades changes this dynamic. It reframes decisions as part of a longer sequence rather than isolated events. Questions shift from "Will this work now?" to "What does this make more likely over time?" Certain paths reveal themselves as dead ends. Others gain significance because their benefits compound. Mental models provide the tools to make these distinctions early, when the cost of adjustment is still low.

This long-view thinking does not eliminate uncertainty. It creates steadiness within it. When you evaluate decisions through multiple lenses and across longer horizons, volatility becomes easier to tolerate. You become less reactive to short-term noise and more attentive to underlying forces. This produces a form of intellectual resilience that is difficult to replicate through effort alone.

A life designed to compound requires more than ambition and execution. It requires judgment that improves with age rather than calcifies. Mental models enable that improvement. Without them, experience accumulates without wisdom. With them, even small decisions begin to align with a coherent direction. The issue was never a lack of effort or intelligence. It was thinking constrained by horizons too short to support lasting clarity.

Over the years, I have adopted a handful of models that shape how I think about my own life.

One is the idea of **first principles**, which asks you to break a problem down to its fundamental truths rather than relying on convention.

Another is **inversion**, a Munger favorite, which encourages you to consider the opposite. What would it take to fail, to regret, to stagnate? Often the clearest path forward emerges by considering what you want to avoid.

A third is **opportunity cost**, the reminder that every choice requires giving up something else. This model forces clarity. It reveals what you value and what you are willing to trade.

These models are not complex. They do not require advanced mathematics or specialized knowledge. What they require is deliberate practice. They become part of how you see the world. They help you evaluate decisions with greater calm and greater confidence. They reduce emotional noise. They sharpen the ability to differentiate between impulse and intention.

Mental models matter most at moments of transition, inflection, or reinvention. The times when a decision cannot be made by instinct alone. The times when thinking clearly matters more than thinking quickly. I felt this during career transitions, during periods of uncertainty, and during moments when I knew the next chapter of my life required a different version of myself. Mental models provided the structure that allowed my thinking to stay steady even when the landscape changed.

At the start of your career, mental models accelerate maturity and decision-making. They help you avoid common errors by teaching you to look beneath the surface. In midlife, they help you navigate complexity and recalibrate assumptions. Later in life, mental models become a way to refine wisdom, a framework for interpreting the patterns of your past and guiding the next chapter.

Mental models do not eliminate uncertainty. They give you the tools to move through uncertainty with clarity. They allow you to remain steady when the world becomes noisy. They create a form of intellectual resilience that compounds. When combined with attention, curiosity, reading, and writing, they form the intellectual infrastructure of a long, well-designed life.

In the end, thinking in decades is not about predicting where you will be far into the future. It is about aligning your decisions with who you want to become. It is about building a worldview that stays intact as life evolves. It is about recognizing that wisdom is not the result of age, but the result of deliberate practices that compound across time.

Mental models are those practices. They are the scaffolding on which long-term clarity is built. And once you begin using them, you begin to see the world and yourself with a level of depth and steadiness that few people ever reach.

CHAPTER 6

The Shape of Exposure

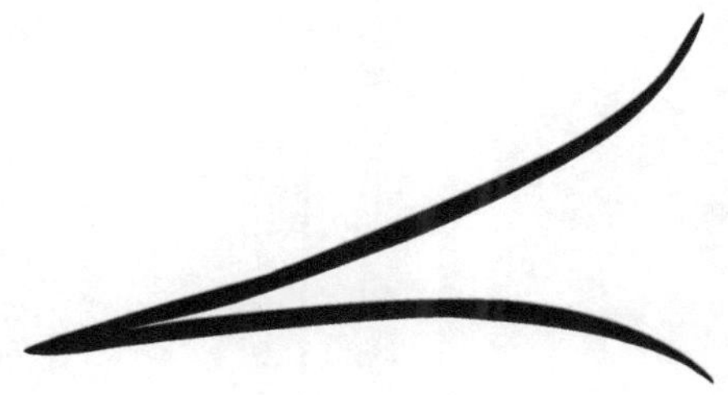

Time rewards what endures stress.

In the previous chapter, we widened the horizon. Thinking in decades changes what feels urgent and what does not. It makes certain tradeoffs look shortsighted and others structurally wise. But time horizon alone is not enough. You can think long-term and still design a life that fractures under stress.

The difference lies in exposure.

Two people can make steady progress for years and arrive at very different outcomes. From the outside, the early slope looks similar—careers advancing, capital accumulating, strength improving. Nothing appears unstable. The divergence becomes visible later, often only after something unexpected happens.

The issue is not effort. It is geometry.

A linear life behaves predictably. Effort produces proportional results. Mistakes cost something, but rarely everything. There is stability in this shape. It bends without collapsing. The limitation is subtle: upside remains bounded by the structure itself.

Fragility presents differently. It often begins with impressive momentum. Leverage accelerates return. Visibility compounds recognition. Productivity feels efficient. Yet fragility is not defined by fluctuation. It reveals itself under stress. A single shock—a financial contraction, a reputational misstep, a health event—can erase years of progress. The trajectory may continue, but from a lower base. Something essential has been permanently altered.

Convexity is quieter. It does not spike early. It is structured so that mistakes are survivable and gains accumulate without being erased. Downside is constrained relative to upside. Risk remains, but it is shaped deliberately.

The distinction is easier to see than to articulate. Over time, lives tend to follow one of several structural payoff shapes.

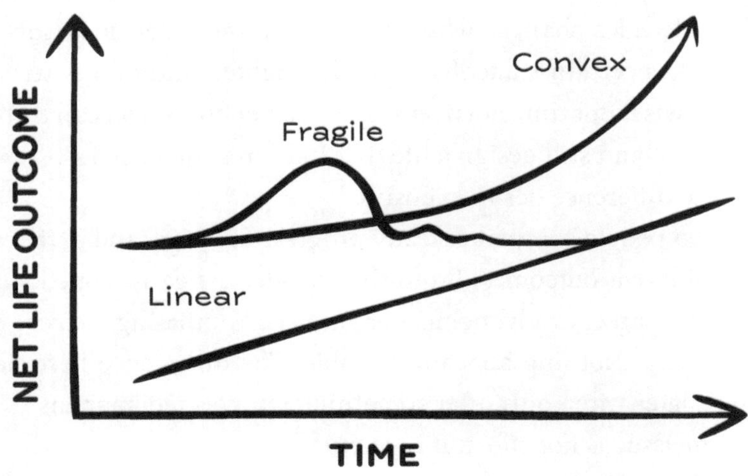

FIGURE 2 The Geometry of Exposure

Early paths often appear identical. Structural differences emerge only under stress. These patterns are not theoretical. I have watched them unfold.

If the language of the long game is to remain useful, it must be precise. Alignment is structural consistency between what you claim matters and what your incentives reward. Drift is the gradual separation between intention and behavior. Design anticipates predictable weakness and reduces its impact in advance. Compounding is the nonlinear accumulation of advantage or disadvantage across time.

Once defined this way, the question becomes practical: where are you exposed?

Intellect becomes fragile when identity fuses with conclusion, when being right matters more than being accurate, and speed is rewarded more than depth. The failure rarely arrives dramatically. It appears as rigidity. Under pressure, thinking narrows.

Capital becomes fragile when leverage exceeds margin, when lifestyle expands faster than resilience, or when too much identity attaches to net worth. I have seen capable people with strong portfolios constrained not by markets, but by fixed obligations they assumed would always remain manageable. Fragility rarely feels reckless in the moment. It feels justified.

Vitality becomes fragile through small neglect. Recovery postponed for another quarter. Sleep traded for one more project. Strength deferred until there is time. The body absorbs these decisions without protest. The consequences often appear later, when reversal is harder.

In each domain, the problem is not ambition. It is exposure to irreversible loss.

Earlier in my career, I focused on reinforcement: build capability, build capital, build network. That orientation works, especially when energy is high and volatility is low. What I came to understand more slowly is that reinforcement alone does not create durability. You can build aggressively and still embed asymmetry that works against you.

I encountered this directly when I left the relative stability of large pharmaceutical work for the volatility of emerging biotech. On paper, the move appeared fragile: smaller balance sheets, narrower margins for error, greater exposure to clinical outcomes and capital markets. The slope of the curve became less predictable. What made the transition survivable was not optimism. It was structure. I had preserved financial margin. I had diversified identity beyond title. I had built relationships that were portable. The risk was real, but it was bounded. Downside would have been uncomfortable, not catastrophic.

The harder discipline is shaping downside before it shapes you.

In intellect, that means holding views lightly enough to revise them without collapse. In capital, it means preferring resilience over marginal yield. In vitality, it means treating recovery as foundational rather than optional.

Convex systems are not immune to stress. They are built to endure it.

Modern life encourages accumulation: more commitments, more exposure, more complexity. Convexity often emerges through subtraction. Removing unnecessary leverage strengthened my capital base more than any allocation shift. Narrowing commitments clarified thinking more than adding another productivity system. Protecting sleep improved performance more reliably than layering supplementation.

None of these adjustments felt dramatic. They were structural, almost invisible in the moment.

Identity carries its own exposure. If identity is concentrated in role, income, or appearance, volatility in those domains destabilizes the whole. I have watched capable leaders struggle at retirement not because they lacked resources, but because their sense of self was overly concentrated. Their capital was diversified. Their identity was not.

A convex identity rests on character, relationships, and capability rather than status alone. It expands with time instead of narrowing around a single role.

The long game, then, is not about steepening the line in the present moment. It is about shaping the curve so that time strengthens rather than erodes it. Linear systems plateau. Fragile systems reset. Convex systems bend gradually and then accelerate.

The divergence is rarely visible early. It becomes obvious only across decades.

Before asking how to grow, it is worth asking where the curve might break. Before optimizing, it is worth examining what could permanently narrow optionality. Before adding, it is worth considering what must be removed.

This isn't pessimism. It's simply maturity.

Compounding works only when the system survives its own stress. Alignment holds only when drift is noticed early. Design matters only when failure modes are acknowledged.

The next chapter turns from geometry to practice. If exposure describes the shape of a life, an operating system determines how that shape is maintained. Convexity does not emerge by accident. It is built deliberately and sustained with discipline.

CHAPTER 7
Building Your Long Game OS

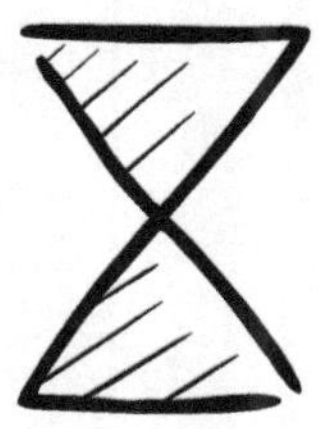

*Insight compounds only
when it is carried forward.*

Over time, it becomes clear that the mind is not designed to hold everything it absorbs. Curiosity opens doors, reading widens your world, and writing brings clarity, but without a way to carry your best ideas forward, much of that understanding fades. You move on to the next task or season, and the insight that once felt sharp begins to blur. A personal operating system is the structure that prevents this slow erosion. It is the quiet architecture that allows your intellect to accumulate rather than reset.

A Long Game OS is not a strict productivity method. It is a way of noticing, preserving, and returning to what matters. It gives continuity to your thinking. It allows understanding to deepen instead of dissipate. It turns the raw material of your life—the books you read, the thoughts you write, the experiences you absorb, and the questions you revisit—into something that endures.

At its core, a Long Game Operating System rests on a few simple principles.

First, it favors depth over volume. The goal is not to capture everything, but to preserve what continues to matter.

Second, it is cyclical rather than linear. Ideas are gathered, developed, revisited, and refined through return. Insight compounds through return, not completion.

Third, it is identity shaping. The ideas you choose to preserve become the lenses through which you see the world and the standards by which you make decisions.

And finally, it is quiet. It operates in the background, strengthening clarity without demanding constant attention.

What makes this a Long Game OS is its relationship with time. It is built to hold ideas for years, not days. To allow questions to remain unresolved. To surface patterns that only reveal themselves across seasons. Most systems are designed for execution. This one is designed for evolution.

The danger of living without a personal operating system is not that you lack intelligence or curiosity. Most people are thoughtful. They read, reflect, and have moments of genuine insight. The cost is that these insights rarely accumulate. Without structure, the mind resets itself again and again, returning to familiar questions as if encountering them for the first time.

This reset is subtle. You may remember having clarity before. You may even recall feeling certain about what mattered. But when insight is not preserved, it loses continuity. Each season feels self-contained. Lessons are relearned rather than built upon. Growth becomes episodic instead of compounding.

The modern environment reinforces this pattern. Information arrives continuously and attention is pulled forward. There is little incentive to return to ideas once they have passed through your awareness. Insight is treated as disposable rather than durable. You read something meaningful, feel its resonance, and then move on. Weeks later, the feeling remains but the structure does not. The idea fades before it can deepen.

This creates a quiet frustration. You sense that you are thinking about the same things you were years ago. The questions persist, but the answers feel incomplete. You know you have grown, yet it is difficult to see how. Without a system to hold your thinking in place, progress becomes difficult to measure and even harder to trust.

This is why people often feel mentally busy but intellectually stagnant. They consume more than they integrate. They gather information without synthesis. Their thinking expands horizontally but not vertically. An operating system exists to solve this problem. It gives your mind memory. It allows insight to persist long enough to evolve.

A personal OS transforms insight from a moment into a

thread. It connects what you are reading now to what mattered before. It allows ideas to mature across time rather than compete for attention in the present. When you revisit a thought months later, you do not start from zero. You resume from where you left off. That continuity is what allows judgment to sharpen and perspective to deepen.

Without this continuity, life becomes more reactive. Decisions are made based on recent inputs rather than accumulated understanding. Patterns are harder to recognize. Direction feels intuitive but fragile. With an OS, decisions rest on a longer internal history. You are less dependent on urgency and more guided by coherence.

The compounding effect here is profound. A system does not make you think more. It makes your thinking stick. Over years, this produces clarity that feels earned rather than forced. You stop chasing insight and begin inhabiting it. The mind becomes steadier because it is no longer required to hold everything at once.

The issue was never a lack of effort or intelligence. It was the absence of a place for insight to live long enough to grow. A Long Game OS corrects that. It turns reflection into structure, structure into memory, and memory into wisdom. This is how thinking begins to compound rather than reset.

In the early stages of adulthood, a system like this accelerates maturity. You are forming a worldview, discovering strengths, absorbing influences, and making decisions that will shape everything that comes next. Without a system, these insights pass quickly. With a system, they accumulate. You begin to see the outline of your intellectual foundation. You start to recognize which ideas endure and which ones fade.

For someone in midlife, an OS serves a different purpose. It becomes a tool for reinvention. Life is no longer a blank slate, but the next chapter may be. You have accumulated decades of experience, but unless those insights are captured and revisited, they remain scattered. A personal OS gathers the fragments of your life into a coherent structure that supports the person you are becoming rather than the person you once were.

The foundation of any OS begins with capture. Ideas rarely arrive on schedule. They surface during walks, workouts, flights, conversations, or moments of stillness. If they are not captured, they disappear. My Moleskine notebook became a simple place to catch these early sparks. It is not a diary or a narrative record. It is a landing place for fragments of thought. Some pages contain a single sentence. Others hold the beginnings of frameworks or questions that deserve attention. These field notes form the first layer of the OS.

Once captured, ideas need space to develop. For this, I use a simple digital structure in Notion. Not because it is elaborate, but because it allows me to revisit and connect what matters. Patterns emerge. Certain themes repeat. Questions return. Books influence one another. Values clarify themselves. None of this came from a master plan. It happened because I created a place for my thoughts to mature instead of being lost to the speed of daily life.

The operating rhythm that sustains this system is simple and repeatable.

Ideas are captured when they appear.

They are developed through writing and reflection.

They are revisited, and meaning deepens.

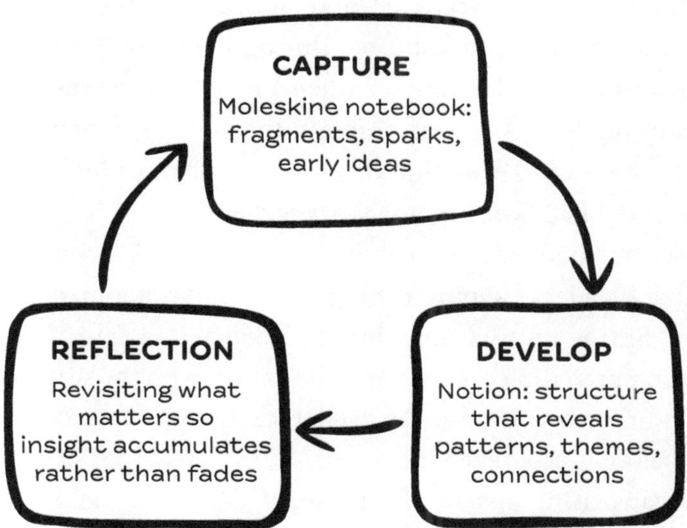

FIGURE 3 The Thinking Loop

Most people capture an idea once and never return to it. But insight compounds only when the mind moves in cycles. Each pass through the loop sharpens the next. Capture strengthens awareness. Development reveals structure. Reflection distills meaning. When you return to the world with clearer insight, you notice more, write better, decide better, and live with greater intention. Nothing here is complicated. That is the point. The long game is built not on volume, but on repetition.

There was a morning when the importance of this became unmistakably clear to me. I was sitting on a bench along the Charles River, the kind of quiet pocket where the city pauses before the day begins. The water was still. Rowers were just beginning to move across the surface. I opened an old Moleskine I had carried across years of travel between Boston and London and began flipping through its pages.

The notes were scattered and informal. Lines written on early flights. Thoughts captured during long days of meetings. Questions I had asked myself when life felt like it was shifting beneath my feet. As I read through those pages, a pattern surfaced. The ideas I was thinking about that morning were the same ones I had been circling years earlier.

The notebook was more than a record. It was a thread, revealing that the ideas I kept returning to were not random, but directional. Sitting on that quiet bench, I realized my thinking had been compounding even when life felt chaotic on the surface. The OS had been working in the background, preserving coherence long before I recognized it.

A surprising benefit of a personal OS is the way it reveals your intellectual lineage. Ideas do not appear in isolation. They come from books that challenged you, experiences that shaped you, and conversations that lingered. An OS allows you to trace where your understanding came from. It shows which ideas grow stronger with time and which ones fade. It reflects your evolution in a way that is invisible when everything remains in your head.

The purpose of an OS is not to store everything. It is to preserve what endures. The questions you return to. The insights that survive distance and time. When revisited across months and years, connections form that could never be forced in the moment. Reading shapes writing. Writing clarifies values. Values improve decisions. Decisions accumulate into better years. In this way, your OS strengthens your trajectory.

In a world of constant input, a personal OS becomes an anchor. Most people consume far more than they integrate. They gather information, but little of it becomes wisdom. A Long Game OS reverses that pattern. It quiets the noise, strengthens the signal, and keeps your mind aligned with what matters most rather than what is simply loud or urgent.

A personal OS also teaches patience. You no longer feel pressure to resolve everything immediately. Questions can remain open. Ideas are allowed to mature. It slows the pace of thought just enough for depth to appear. Clarity becomes something you cultivate rather than something you chase.

Your OS does not need to be complex. It needs to be consistent. A place to capture. A place to develop. A rhythm of returning. And the humility to notice which ideas continue to shape your life. This simple structure becomes one of the most powerful forces in your life. It becomes the bridge between your past and your future, the place where wisdom accumulates and clarity deepens.

In the end, The Long Game OS is not about tools or templates. It is about giving your mind a place to grow. It preserves what matters, strengthens the thinking that notices it, and ensures that the best parts of your intellectual life are never lost. In a world optimized for speed, it protects meaning and allows insight to compound across a lifetime.

PART II
CAPITAL

Wealth as Freedom,
Stewardship, and Optionality

CHAPTER 8

Rethinking Wealth:
What Money Is Actually For

Wealth is not an outcome.
It is infrastructure for freedom.

Most people think building wealth is complicated. They imagine it requires advanced mathematics, perfect timing, sophisticated models, or an insider's understanding of the markets. They assume wealth is the reward for exceptional intelligence or access. But the longer I have lived, the more I have seen the opposite. True wealth has very little to do with complexity. It has even less to do with cleverness. Wealth is built through simplicity, patience, and restraint.

I began learning this long before I had any meaningful money to manage. I was twenty-three, fresh out of college, standing at the edge of adulthood and trying to imagine what my future might look like. One evening, I picked up a book that would shape the way I thought about wealth for decades. *The Millionaire Next Door* was not glamorous. It did not promise secrets or shortcuts. It simply described the lives of people who had built real financial independence through discipline, restraint, and an almost old-fashioned sense of practicality.

I remember sitting in my bedroom, the kind of space filled with mismatched furniture and the remnants of student life, and feeling something shift. The book was describing a kind of success I had never seen up close but instinctively understood. Wealth, it suggested, was not the result of luck or brilliance. It was the product of simple habits repeated consistently. It belonged to people who lived below their means, protected their time, avoided unnecessary risks, and built a margin around their lives.

At twenty-three, I did not have much to manage financially, but I had something far more valuable. I had a clean slate. I had the ability to choose what kind of life I wanted to build. That book gave me a framework that would guide almost every major financial decision I made in the years ahead. It taught me that wealth was not about appearing successful. It was about creating optionality. It was about designing a life where the future was not determined by the demands of the present.

I did not know it then, but that evening became the beginning of my long game.

The truth is that wealth buys something far more meaningful than lifestyle. It buys freedom. The freedom to choose the work that aligns with who you are becoming. The freedom to step away from environments that no longer fit. The freedom to think clearly without the fog of financial anxiety. The freedom to move toward the life you want instead of the life you feel pressured into living.

When you see wealth through this lens, the architecture of it becomes almost obvious. It grows out of how you structure your life, not how you outperform others. It is shaped by the habits you repeat, not the predictions you make. It is strengthened by the decisions you avoid as much as the ones you pursue. And it is protected by a single question that sits beneath every financial choice: Does this increase or decrease the freedom of my future self?

When you begin to view wealth this way, the noise around money falls away. Urgency disappears. Status loses meaning. Money becomes less of a scoreboard and more of a buffer. It becomes something you steward rather than chase. And it becomes a tool that supports the life you want rather than a force that pulls you into a life you never intended.

The danger of misunderstanding wealth is not that it leads to obvious financial mistakes. Most people save, invest, and make generally sensible choices. The cost is subtler. When wealth is treated as an end rather than a means, it reshapes behavior. Decisions begin to optimize for accumulation instead of alignment. Money becomes something to protect rather than something that protects you.

This shift often happens gradually. Early wins reinforce the idea that more is always better. Progress is measured numerically rather than experientially. Net worth grows, but clarity does not. Without a clear definition of what wealth is for, accumulation becomes reflexive. You keep playing the game because you are winning, even if the game no longer serves the life you want.

The environment reinforces this confusion. Financial culture celebrates growth without context. Rankings, benchmarks, and comparisons are everywhere. Success is framed as outperformance rather than sufficiency. It becomes easy to confuse motion with meaning. Wealth becomes a scoreboard rather than a stabilizer.

When this happens, optionality begins to narrow rather than expand. Commitments multiply. Fixed costs rise. Psychological attachment to a certain standard of living hardens. Ironically, the very thing meant to create freedom starts to create fragility. You may be financially successful and still feel constrained, not because you lack resources, but because your wealth was never anchored to intention.

This is why so many people experience unease at precisely the moment they are "doing well." The numbers say progress, but something feels off. The issue is not ingratitude or ambition. It is misalignment. Wealth that is not designed to support a specific vision of life defaults to supporting external expectations instead.

Clarity restores balance. When you define what wealth is for, accumulation becomes directional rather than compulsive. Decisions become simpler. Trade-offs become visible. You begin to evaluate choices not by whether they increase your net worth, but by whether they strengthen your autonomy, resilience, and capacity to choose well across decades.

This reframing also changes risk tolerance. You become less interested in chasing upside and more focused on protecting trajectory. Catastrophic loss matters more than incremental gain. Stability becomes a feature rather than a constraint. You recognize that wealth compounds best when it is allowed to remain boring and durable.

Importantly, redefining wealth does not require withdrawal or minimalism. It requires coherence. Wealth can support ambition, creativity, and growth when it is aligned with values rather than vanity. The difference is not how much you have, but how intentionally it is structured. Wealth that serves a clear purpose simplifies life. Wealth without one complicates it.

This clarity produces a different relationship with money. Anxiety decreases. Comparison loses its grip. You begin to see money less as a measure of success and more as infrastructure. Something that runs in the background, enabling the parts of life that matter most to remain stable and well supported.

The mistake was never wanting more. It was never striving. The mistake was allowing accumulation to outrun intention. When wealth is reconnected to purpose, it regains its power. It stops pulling you forward blindly and begins supporting you steadily. That is when wealth becomes what it was always meant to be: a quiet enabler of a life designed on your terms.

The core of simple wealth is built on three ideas. The first is **alignment**. Your financial life must support the life you want, not the life others expect of you. Alignment is what prevents lifestyle drift, unnecessary obligations, and commitments that erode your autonomy. When your finances and your values are pointed in the same direction, everything becomes lighter. You spend less energy managing contradictions and more energy living intentionally.

The second is **protection**. Wealth is most fragile during periods of transition, distraction, and emotional decision-making.

The world rewards urgency, but wealth rewards patience. A simple architecture reduces the number of decisions you need to make. It limits exposure to the unpredictable. It allows compounding to work uninterrupted and consistently. Protection is not about fear. It is about designing your financial life so that time becomes your ally.

The third is **optionality**. Real freedom is not found in consumption. It is found in the ability to choose how you spend your time. Optionality allows you to say no without anxiety. It gives you room to reorient your life without destabilizing it. It makes reinvention possible. Wealth that cannot adapt is not wealth. It is dependency. Wealth that expands your optionality is the foundation of a life that compounds.

For most people, the challenge is not learning what to do. It is learning what to ignore. The financial world thrives on complexity because complexity keeps people dependent. It is easier to sell strategies that sound advanced than ones based on simplicity and discipline. Yet almost every meaningful financial decision can be rendered through a small number of principles: spend less than you earn, avoid unnecessary debt, invest consistently, focus on ownership, protect against catastrophic loss, and let compounding work across decades.

Simple does not mean easy. Simplicity requires clarity. It requires resisting distraction. It requires a willingness to build slowly rather than chase shortcuts. But simplicity is durable. It survives economic cycles, changing fashions, and shifting opinions. It is the architecture that has rewarded disciplined people for generations.

For someone in their twenties, simple wealth creates an extraordinary opportunity. It allows compounding to begin early, long before income peaks or responsibilities multiply. It replaces anxiety with direction. It removes the pressure to guess what the future will look like and offers a framework that works regardless of specific outcomes. At this stage, wealth buys possibility and the confidence you are on the right path.

For someone in midlife, simple wealth becomes stabilization. It allows you to recalibrate, redesign your life, and make decisions based on alignment rather than fear. It quiets the noise of comparison. It reminds you that the goal is not to win a race, but to build a life that feels congruent with who you are becoming. At this stage, wealth buys resilience.

For someone later in life, simplicity becomes legacy. It allows you to pass on clarity rather than confusion. It provides structure rather than burden. It helps those you care about understand not just what you built, but why you built it. At this stage, wealth buys continuity.

The truth is that most people overestimate what cleverness can do and underestimate what consistency can do. They chase complexity when they need simplicity. They look for breakthroughs when what they need is patience. Wealth rarely arrives in dramatic moments. It accumulates gradually, in the background of a life lived intentionally.

The simple architecture of wealth is not a strategy. It is a posture. It is a long-term orientation. It is the willingness to let time work on your behalf. When you build your financial life around clarity, patience, and protection, everything else becomes easier.

Wealth becomes less about achieving something extraordinary and more about avoiding the mistakes that prevent compounding from doing its work. It becomes less about predicting the future and more about preparing for it. And it becomes less about accumulation and more about alignment.

In the end, wealth is not about money. It is about autonomy. It is about being able to choose the life you want and move toward it with intention. When you understand what wealth truly buys, you begin to build it differently. You begin to build it deliberately, with a sense of purpose that lasts.

CHAPTER 9
Becoming (and Staying) Wealthy

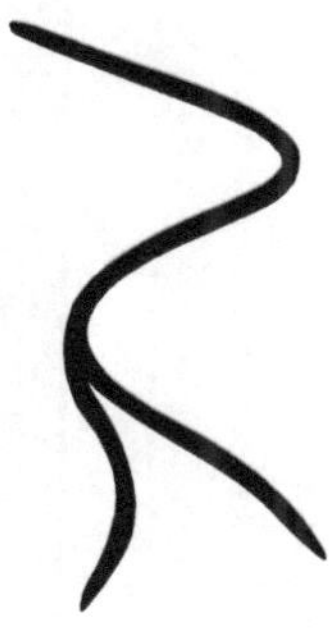

*Wealth is built with discipline
and preserved with restraint.*

Wealth is often misunderstood. Many people think it begins with income, talent, luck, or opportunity. But becoming wealthy, and staying wealthy, has far more to do with behavior than with numbers. Financial outcomes are shaped less by what you earn and more by how you think, how you decide, and how you steady yourself when the world around you becomes noisy.

The habits that build wealth are simple. The discipline to maintain them is rare. Becoming wealthy is a challenge. Staying wealthy is a practice.

That understanding began earlier than I realized at the time. While in college, I enrolled in a course on estate and retirement planning that left an impression far beyond its syllabus. The professor's quiet refrain, *invest early, stay the course, let time work*, lodged itself deeply. I still keep the notebook from that class, and every so often, I flip through its worn pages, a tangible reminder that the simplest lessons often prove the most enduring.

And that perspective took shape long before I encountered spreadsheets or investment books. It began with a moment that felt small at the time but became foundational in hindsight.

A few years later, I remember receiving my first real promotion in my mid-twenties. The title was modest, but to me, it felt like a step into adulthood. After work, I stopped by a bookstore. I wandered through the business section without much direction until I came across a slim paperback on advanced Excel modeling. At that stage of my career, I was an analyst trying to sharpen my skills, convinced that better models would make me better at the work.

I sat on a comfortable leather chair between the shelves and started reading. Some time passed before I even looked up. What struck me, though, was not the formulas or techniques. It was the underlying idea woven through the examples. Great analysts were not defined by clever spreadsheets. They were defined by clarity of thinking. They knew what mattered. They made disciplined assumptions. They favored simplicity over flash. They understood that precision meant nothing without judgment.

That moment taught me something I did not yet have the language for: the habits that make you effective in work are often the same habits that make you effective with money. Clarity over complexity. Judgment over theatrics. Structure over impulse. Wealth, like great analysis, is built on the quiet discipline of getting the fundamentals right. It grows when you simplify what matters, remove what does not, and make decisions that support your future rather than impress your present. The lesson had nothing to do with spreadsheets and everything to do with behavior. And behavior, left unattended, has a way of drifting.

The greatest threat to wealth is not market crashes, recessions, or bad luck. Those events are visible and often temporary. The more common danger is behavioral drift. Wealth is rarely lost in a single dramatic moment. It erodes gradually, through small decisions made without reflection, especially during periods when life feels busy, successful, or secure.

There was a period when this distinction became personal. A portion of my portfolio had been allocated to an emerging markets investment, recommended as a way to improve returns through diversification and exposure to faster-growing economies. The case was familiar and persuasive. On paper, it promised higher returns and a more refined allocation. In practice, the benefit never fully showed up. Performance was uneven, while the complexity was constant. The position required monitoring, explanation, and a level of attention that felt out of proportion to what it actually delivered. Exiting it meant letting go of a promise rather than a result. That decision proved right. Simplifying the portfolio removed friction without sacrificing outcomes. It made the portfolio easier to understand, easier to hold through volatility, and easier to leave alone. What I learned was not a lesson about emerging markets or any single investment, but about judgment. Complexity that does not clearly earn its place eventually taxes judgment. Simplicity, by contrast, compounds by reducing the number of decisions that can pull you off course.

That experience clarified something I have seen repeatedly. The real work of staying wealthy is not finding better ideas, but building a structure that makes it easier to behave well over long stretches of time. A portfolio that is simple enough to understand is easier to trust. One that is easy to trust is easier to hold. And one that is easy to hold is far more likely to compound. The enemy at this stage is not ignorance. It is restlessness. The quiet urge to adjust, refine, or optimize what is already working. Over decades, resisting that urge matters more than any incremental improvement you might capture by indulging it.

As income rises, that restlessness is often given room to express itself. Not because of extravagance, but because expectations expand gradually. Homes become larger. Commitments become longer-term. Fixed costs accumulate. Each decision feels reasonable on its own. Together, they reduce flexibility. Optionality narrows not with alarm, but with comfort.

This is why staying wealthy is often harder than becoming wealthy. Early discipline is reinforced by necessity. Later discipline must be sustained voluntarily. When resources are abundant, the consequences of small mistakes are delayed. The feedback loop weakens. What once required intention begins to run on autopilot.

The environment makes this harder. Social comparison intensifies as success becomes visible. Professional circles normalize higher spending. Lifestyle inflation is framed as progress. It becomes difficult to distinguish between what you can afford and what you should carry. Wealth shifts from being a buffer to being a responsibility that demands maintenance.

Risk also changes character as wealth grows. Early risks are often constructive: investing in skills, careers, or opportunities that increase earning power. Later risks tend to be asymmetric. They offer limited upside and disproportionate downside. Yet confidence bred from past success can obscure this shift. People mistake familiarity with markets or business for immunity from loss.

Emotional decision-making compounds the danger. Wealth magnifies the consequences of acting on fear, excitement, or ego. Chasing returns after periods of underperformance. Overreacting to volatility. Making investments to feel sophisticated rather than to serve a clear purpose. These behaviors do not reflect ignorance. They reflect temperament under pressure.

Staying wealthy requires a different mindset than becoming wealthy. It favors preservation over acceleration. It prioritizes margin over maximization. It values resilience more than optimization. This does not mean avoiding growth. It means respecting fragility. Wealth compounds best when it is allowed to remain boring, diversified, and structurally protected.

Clarity restores discipline. When you are clear about what wealth is for, restraint becomes easier. Decisions are evaluated through their impact on long-term autonomy rather than short-term satisfaction. You become more willing to say no, not because you cannot afford something, but because you choose not to carry it.

The paradox is that restraint often increases satisfaction. A life with fewer financial obligations offers more psychological space. Fewer dependencies create more freedom. Wealth regains its original purpose as a stabilizing force rather than a source of complexity.

Most fortunes are lost not through ignorance, but through neglect. Not through ambition, but through drift. The discipline that builds wealth must evolve into the wisdom that protects it. When that transition is made deliberately, wealth becomes durable. When it is ignored, even significant resources can become fragile.

Becoming wealthy teaches you what is possible. Staying wealthy teaches you what matters. The long game depends on mastering both.

The first is driven by behavior. The second is sustained by temperament. As income rises, expectations shift, and life grows more complex, wealth depends less on intelligence and more on the ability to remain steady.

To become wealthy, you must first live below your means. It is simple in theory and surprisingly difficult in practice. It requires resisting the temptation to match the pace, possessions, or expectations of others. It requires clarity about what matters to you and indifference toward what does not. It requires patience when others are impatient and discipline when others are improvising.

To stay wealthy, you must protect yourself from the two forces that erode fortunes more reliably than anything else: unnecessary risk and emotional decision-making. That means avoiding obligations that narrow future freedom and building buffers that absorb the unexpected. Your financial life should be designed so that the inevitable downturns of markets or life do not break you. Staying wealthy is far more about avoiding mistakes than chasing returns.

Wealth compounds insofar as it is protected from unnecessary fragility.

That protection does not stop at the portfolio. It extends to life itself. Adequate health insurance protects the financial foundation from medical shocks that can undo decades of disciplined saving. Thoughtfully structured life insurance protects the people who depend on you from sudden absence. These decisions are rarely exciting. They do not compound visibly. But they preserve optionality and prevent fragility. In the long game, avoiding catastrophic setbacks matters as much as pursuing growth.

Before going further, it helps to see the distinction clearly. Wealth is not a single skill but two disciplines. The first is becoming wealthy: the habits that build the foundation. The second is staying wealthy: the behaviors that protect it. Most people master one and overlook the other. The long game requires both.

The Two Halves of Wealth

BECOMING	STAYING
• Live below your means	• Maintain a buffer
• Stay patient and disciplined	• Simplify your finances
• Avoid unnecessary risks	• Protect your independence

FIGURE 4 Becoming Wealthy vs. Staying Wealthy

The two halves of wealth are simple, but not symmetrical. One is built through ambition, the other through restraint. Together, they shape a financial life that endures.

For someone in their twenties, becoming wealthy begins with habits. Saving early. Building skills. Investing consistently. Creating optionality through simple financial decisions that compound. These aren't impressive in the moment, but they build a foundation others will envy later.

For someone in midlife, staying wealthy becomes the priority. This is the season where careers peak, lifestyles expand, families grow, and complexity increases. The danger is drift. Spending accelerates unconsciously. Obligations accumulate. The margin for error narrows. In this phase, restraint becomes more important than ambition. Stability matters more than spectacle. Protection carries more weight than risk.

For someone later in life, staying wealthy becomes legacy. Not legacy in the sense of accumulation, but in the sense of clarity. It means simplifying finances, protecting independence, and ensuring that the resources you have built support your life rather than complicate it. It is the transition from building wealth to preserving autonomy.

Becoming wealthy requires discipline and habit. Staying wealthy requires wisdom and restraint.

The quiet truth is that wealth grows best in calm environments. It compounds when you do not disturb it. It strengthens when you avoid unnecessary exposure. It expands when your life is aligned with your values. Most financial problems are not caused by lack of knowledge, but by lack of consistency. Most financial successes come from staying the course when others are reacting emotionally.

Wealth is built over decades, not years. It is shaped by temperament, not luck. It is protected through simplicity, not complexity. Becoming wealthy is about doing the right things early. Staying wealthy is about continuing to do them long after the world tells you that you no longer need to.

In the end, wealth is less about achieving something extraordinary and more about avoiding the avoidable. It is the quiet combination of patience, clarity, and behavior. It is the practice of strengthening your life rather than signaling it. It is the alignment between your financial decisions and the person you want to become.

Becoming wealthy gives you freedom.

Staying wealthy keeps it.

CHAPTER 10

A Durable Portfolio

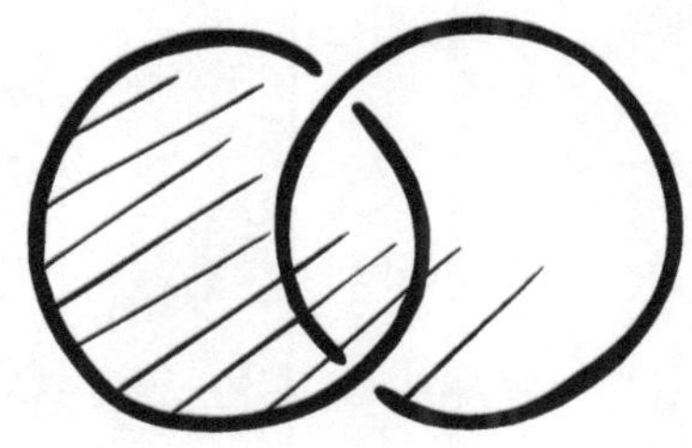

*The best portfolios are
the ones you can sustain.*

Investing is one of the few areas of life where complexity consistently underperforms simplicity. People assume that more information, more opinions, and more sophistication lead to better results. Yet almost every study of long-term returns tells a different story. The portfolios that succeed across decades are not the clever ones. They are the ones people can stick with. They are the ones built on clarity, not prediction. They are the ones designed thoughtfully rather than engineered anxiously.

My understanding of this came slowly, shaped by experience more than theory. There was a period midway through my career when the principle revealed itself with uncomfortable clarity. My portfolio reflected my life—sophisticated on paper, fragmented in practice.

I was living in Zurich then, working across EMEA and moving constantly between countries, teams, and strategic priorities. The calendar was full and the responsibilities real. From the outside, it looked like momentum. But momentum and alignment are not the same thing.

One evening, after a long week of meetings, I returned to my flat on Weinbergstrasse. The city was quiet. I sat at the kitchen table that had become my unofficial planning desk and opened my laptop to review my accounts. I had been investing for two decades, but my approach had become fragmented. A mix of U.S. and international funds. A few thematic ideas and several allocations suggested by my financial advisor, particularly in emerging markets, offered with far more conviction than I felt.

For over a decade, I had worked with a financial advisor who helped me navigate corporate equity, pensions, and cross-border tax planning during my years abroad. The guidance mattered. But the portfolio grew more complex than necessary. Fees compounded invisibly. The structure became harder to explain in a sentence. Nothing failed. But clarity thinned.

Looking at my portfolio that evening, I felt something like tension. Not fear, not confusion, but a sense that I was creating more noise than progress. On instinct, I revisited a long-term investing framework I had saved months earlier. It made an argument so simple I almost dismissed it: Most people should own broad market exposure through a single low-cost index fund and pair it with the right amount of bonds for stability. Nothing more. No forecasting. No performance chasing. No added complexity.

That night, in a flat far from home, I simplified. I shifted the majority of my holdings into a broad-based S&P 500 index fund, paired it with a modest bond allocation, and removed everything that created friction or doubt. I did not know it then, but that decision would shape my financial trajectory for the decades to come. It freed my attention. It created consistency. It allowed compounding to work without my interference.

Portfolio design is not about finding the perfect strategy. It is about choosing an approach you can follow through every season of the market. The most powerful portfolios are the ones that remove the need for constant decisions. They protect you from your own impulses. They turn investing into a system rather than a series of reactions.

The greatest mistake in portfolio design is assuming that markets are the primary source of risk. Over long periods, markets tend to reward ownership. The more significant risk lies elsewhere: in the investor's behavior under stress. Portfolios rarely fail because they were poorly constructed. They fail because they were impossible to live with.

Complex portfolios create hidden pressure. Each additional allocation introduces a decision point. Each thematic bet adds a reason to second-guess. Each deviation from the core invites comparison. This complexity demands attention.

It asks to be monitored, adjusted, defended, and explained. That attention is costly. It pulls focus away from the long-term and toward the immediate.

This is why complexity feels sophisticated but behaves fragile. It performs best in calm environments and worst when clarity is most needed. During volatility, complex portfolios generate conflicting signals. Some components rise while others fall. Rationalizations multiply. The temptation to intervene grows stronger. What began as diversification becomes distraction.

Simplicity works differently. A simple portfolio narrows the number of decisions you need to make. It reduces the surface area for error. It allows you to experience volatility without interpreting it as instruction. When markets fall, the question is not "Which part failed?" but simply "Can I stay the course?" That single question is far easier to answer.

The real advantage of a well-designed portfolio is not return maximization. It is decision minimization. The fewer choices required during periods of stress, the more likely you are to behave well. Good behavior compounds. Poor behavior compounds just as powerfully in the opposite direction.

This distinction becomes more important as wealth grows. Early in life, mistakes are recoverable. Time absorbs them. Later, the margin for error narrows. A portfolio that invites emotional responses becomes dangerous precisely when stability matters most. Simplicity becomes not just elegant, but protective.

Designing a portfolio you can live with requires honesty about temperament. Some people are comfortable with volatility. Others are not. Neither is superior. The mistake is borrowing someone else's tolerance rather than understanding your own. A portfolio that matches your psychological wiring will outperform a theoretically superior one you cannot maintain.

This is why alignment matters more than optimization. A portfolio aligned with your life stage, income stability, and emotional disposition allows compounding to work uninterrupted. It becomes background infrastructure rather than a source of ongoing engagement. The best portfolios are almost boring by design.

Over decades, this boredom becomes an advantage. You stop reacting. You stop chasing. You stop needing the market to validate your intelligence. Investing becomes a steady practice rather than a recurring test of nerve. That steadiness is what allows wealth to accumulate without drama.

The irony is that the simplest portfolios often feel the hardest to adopt. They offer no narrative. No excitement. No sense of cleverness. What they offer instead is durability. And durability is what wins across a lifetime.

The classic 90/10 portfolio is the simplest expression of this philosophy: 90 percent in broad equity ownership, 10 percent in high-quality bonds. You participate fully in the long-term growth of productive companies while maintaining a small cushion that smooths volatility. Elegant in its simplicity, it offers more than most investors will ever need.

But portfolio design is not static. Just as your life evolves, your portfolio should evolve with it. A twenty-three-year-old with decades ahead of them can afford market swings that would feel destabilizing later in life. A fifty-five-year-old with a clear sense of their long-term direction may prefer something steadier, like a 70/30 or 60/40 blend. This shift is not about fear. It is about alignment. Design your portfolio so it matches both your temperament and your stage of life.

For someone in their twenties, the goal is to begin simply and begin early. A portfolio anchored in ownership rather than speculation gives compounding time to do the heavy lifting. Markets will rise and fall, but the discipline of consistent investing through every environment is what builds real wealth. You are not trying to be clever. You are trying to be durable.

For someone in their fifties, the priority becomes avoiding late-game mistakes. Complexity creates fragility. Emotion creates risk. The temptation to chase trends or protect against imaginary threats becomes costly. A simpler portfolio does not just reduce stress. It reduces behavioral errors. It keeps you aligned with your long-term plan rather than the opinions of the moment.

A portfolio designed to endure across a lifetime has three qualities. It is simple enough to understand. It is stable enough to withstand volatility. It is structured enough to prevent your emotions from making decisions that your future self will regret. It offers clarity instead of noise. It strengthens your position instead of complicating it. It allows you to stay the course when others are reacting.

It's not built on prediction, optimization, or complexity. It's built on structure. The key is to design an allocation that compounds in the background, absorbs shocks, preserves optionality, and leaves room for thoughtful discretion. What follows is the architecture I've found most enduring. A simple, repeatable system that keeps your long-term engine running while protecting your ability to stay invested through every season of the market.

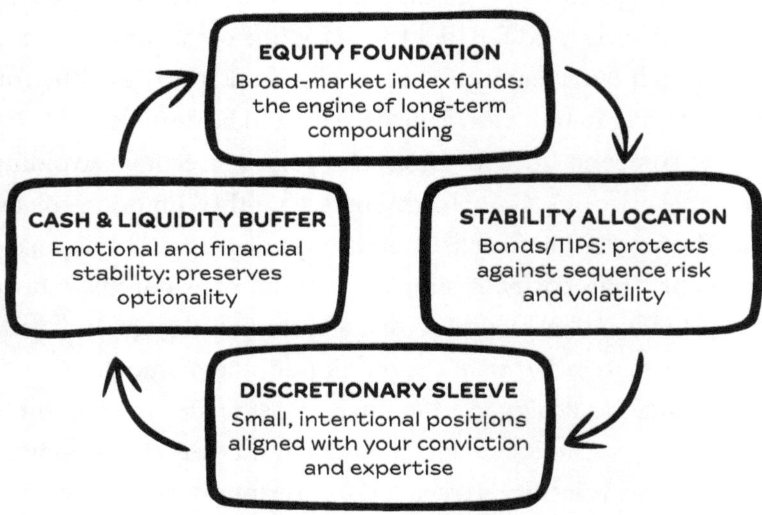

FIGURE 5 The Power of a Simple Portfolio

When these elements work together, the portfolio becomes something sturdier than a collection of holdings. It becomes a system. One that compounds steadily, protects you from the predictable shocks of the market, and allows for thoughtful expression without jeopardizing the foundation. The goal isn't to outperform the market. The goal is to build an approach you can stay committed to for the rest of your life. A durable portfolio is ultimately one you can hold through noise, through cycles, and through every changing season of your own life.

In the end, the most successful portfolios are not those that look impressive on a spreadsheet. They are the ones that reliably support the life you want to build. They give you stability. They give you resilience. They give you optionality. And they allow you to move through your financial life with calm rather than urgency.

Simplicity is not a compromise. It is a strength. And in the long game, it is a decisive advantage.

CHAPTER 11
The Micro Family Office Blueprint

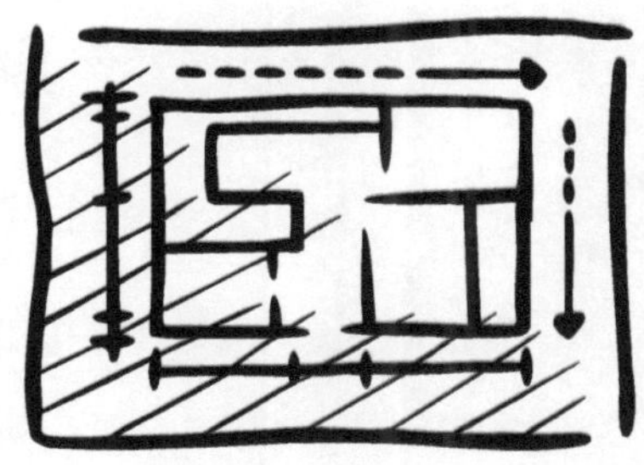

Complexity doesn't arrive all at once.
It accumulates.

At a certain point, as wealth grows, so does complexity. Accounts accumulate. Decisions stretch across years instead of months. Risks become less about income and more about structure. Money stops being something you manage and becomes something you steward. Many people reach this stage without realizing they have crossed a threshold. They continue making decisions the way they always have. They react instead of design. They optimize instead of organize. That is when complexity begins to compound faster than assets.

A micro family office is not a building, a staff, or a formal entity. It is a mindset. It is a personal operating system for your financial life. It turns wealth from something that pulls at your attention into something that supports it. It gives you clarity, structure, and rhythm. It allows you to move through your financial life intentionally rather than reactively. And it gives you the ability to plan decades ahead without being overwhelmed by the details.

My understanding of this began during a quiet afternoon at home. I was sitting in my study, a room lined with books collected across years of reading and travel, overlooking the calm of the woods outside. The light had settled into that late-day stillness that invites reflection. I opened my laptop to review one of my financial summaries, something I had done countless times before, but that afternoon it felt different. I began listing out everything I was managing retirement accounts, brokerage accounts, insurance policies, real estate, liquidity, long-term planning. Nothing was chaotic, yet the structure felt loose. It felt like an operating system built through years of momentum rather than years of intention.

As I looked at the list, I realized that the problem wasn't the assets themselves. The problem was the absence of a cohesive system that could hold them. Complexity had accumulated gradually, the way clutter fills a room you stop noticing. That moment in my study made something clear: it was time to elevate the way I approached my financial life. It was time to build a framework capable of absorbing complexity without amplifying it. It was time to operate with a micro family office mindset.

This moment is not unusual. It is structural. The hidden risk of growing wealth is not mismanagement. It is drift. Systems that were sufficient at one stage of life become strained at the next, not because anything broke, but because nothing evolved. Decisions multiply. Accounts fragment. Advisors speak in silos. Without intention, structure lags behind scale.

This is how complexity takes control. You still feel responsible. You still review statements. But your financial life begins to operate as a collection of parts rather than a coherent whole. Each decision requires more energy. Each change carries unintended consequences. Attention is consumed by maintenance rather than direction.

The purpose of a micro family office is not to create sophistication. It is to reclaim simplicity at a higher level. It replaces reactive decision-making with design. It ensures that growth strengthens coherence rather than eroding it. When structure is absent, wealth creates noise. When structure is present, wealth creates stability.

Most people wait too long to formalize their financial life because everything appears manageable—until it no longer is. By the time friction becomes obvious, the system is already working against them. The opportunity cost is not just inefficiency. It is attention diverted away from the parts of life that matter most.

A micro family office mindset anticipates this transition. It treats structure as an investment rather than an administrative burden. It acknowledges that clarity must scale alongside assets.

And it accepts that the greatest risk at higher levels of wealth is not poor returns, but poor coordination.

This coordination matters because financial decisions are rarely isolated. Tax strategy affects investment strategy. Liquidity affects risk tolerance. Estate planning affects asset location. Without a unifying framework, optimization in one area can create fragility in another. A micro family office exists to resolve these tensions before they become problems.

Importantly, this mindset is not about control. It is about reducing cognitive load. When your financial life is well designed, fewer decisions require real-time judgment. Defaults are clear. Principles are explicit. Trade-offs are understood in advance. This frees mental energy for higher-order thinking and living.

The deeper benefit is psychological. Structure creates calm. It replaces background anxiety with quiet confidence. You stop wondering whether something important has been overlooked. You know where everything lives, why it exists, and how it connects. That clarity compounds just as powerfully as capital.

A micro family office also changes how you interact with advisors. Instead of reacting to recommendations, you evaluate them against your framework. Advice becomes input rather than direction. You move from delegation to stewardship. This shift alone prevents countless small mistakes that accumulate.

The goal is not to build something impressive. It is to build something durable. A structure that works when life is busy. When markets are volatile. When decisions carry more weight. When your attention is better spent elsewhere. Wealth should simplify your life as it grows, not complicate it.

This is why the micro family office is best understood as an operating system rather than a solution. It does not eliminate complexity. It absorbs it. It ensures that growth strengthens alignment instead of eroding it. And it allows wealth to support the life you want rather than quietly demanding more from it.

From that foundation flow its three core purposes: to create clarity, build systems, and protect your future self. It is the opposite of improvisation. It is the decision to treat your financial life with the same seriousness, calm, and professionalism that you would bring to an important enterprise. What matters isn't scale, but stewardship—designing a structure that reduces friction so your time can be spent where it actually makes life richer.

One of the most essential elements of this mindset is the creation of a few strategic documents. These documents are not administrative tasks. They are instruments of clarity. They reduce emotional decision-making and anchor your choices to long-term direction.

The first is a set of **Family Office Principles**. These are not meant to inspire. They are meant to clarify. A single page that reflects how you intend to approach money across your life. Simplicity. Stewardship. Restraint. These principles do not change often. They are the foundation.

The second is your **Investment Philosophy and Plan**. It outlines how you invest, why you invest that way, and what you intentionally ignore. Markets will always test discipline. This document holds it in place. It protects decades of progress from the impulses caused by market volatility.

The third is a **Liquidity Policy**. This may be the most underrated document. It defines how much cash you hold and what that cash is for. Liquidity is not just a financial buffer. It is an emotional buffer. It is the structure that allows calm decisions during turbulent times.

The fourth is an **Estate Plan**. Not because you are focused on legacy in the traditional sense, but because clarity is a form of care. An estate plan ensures that the people you care about inherit order rather than confusion. It prevents stress at a moment when clarity matters most.

Together, these documents create structure without creating complexity. They provide a rhythm for your financial life. They reduce the friction of constant reevaluation. They keep you aligned with the person you are becoming rather than the emotions of the moment. They transform wealth from something you must constantly monitor into something that strengthens your life.

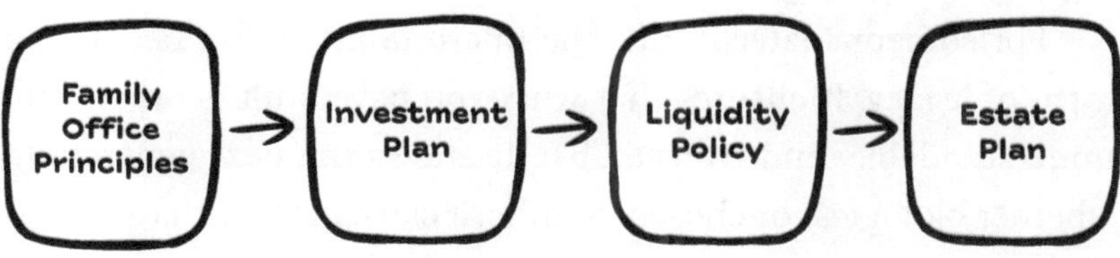

FIGURE 6 The Four Pillars of Stewardship

These four pillars create more than structure; they create a posture. When they are in place, your financial life becomes quieter, clearer, and less reactive. Decisions stop happening in isolation and begin flowing from a coherent structure. You are no longer relying on willpower or instinct in moments of stress; you are relying on design. Their purpose is not bureaucracy. The purpose is alignment between your values, your behavior, and your long-term direction. With this structure established, each document becomes a stabilizing force, anchoring the rest of your financial life.

For someone starting out in life, the micro family office mindset is an early advantage. It teaches you to treat money with intention before complexity enters the picture. Setting up simple systems early multiplies their effect. A young person who learns to steward small amounts will one day steward larger amounts with clarity rather than surprise.

For someone in midlife, this mindset becomes essential. This is the stage where wealth becomes multidimensional. Investments develop histories. Property requires oversight. Retirement planning becomes concrete. Taxes become real. Responsibilities expand. Without structure, these areas begin competing for attention. They create noise. They create stress. They create risk. A micro family office transforms that noise into order. It consolidates. It simplifies. It brings everything under one coherent system.

For someone later in life, the micro family office becomes a form of legacy. It ensures that what you have built is organized, understandable, and transferable. It allows the next generation, whether biological or chosen, to inherit clarity rather than confusion. It passes down not only resources but values. It signals that wealth is not an identity but a responsibility.

In the end, a micro family office is not about money. It is about alignment. It is about moving through your financial life with intention rather than drift. It is about reducing chaos so that you can devote your best attention to health, relationships, purpose, and the things that make life meaningful.

A micro family office is a simple idea. It is the decision to operate with clarity and care. And it becomes something far more profound. It becomes the quiet structure that supports everything else. It becomes the foundation of a life that compounds.

CHAPTER 12

Income Stacking Across a Lifetime

*Income becomes powerful when
it is arranged, not maximized.*

Over the course of a life, income shifts. It begins as something linear and fragile, dependent on your time and your presence. Later, it becomes something quieter, something more varied and more stable. Income broadens. It gains depth. It begins to compound. And eventually, if designed well, it becomes a structure that supports your life with far less effort than it once required.

Income stacking is the art of arranging these layers so they reinforce one another. Not in a short-term tactical sense, but in a structural one. It is the transition from seeing income as a single stream to seeing it as a portfolio of cash flows that operate together across decades. It is the quiet foundation that allows your long game to become self-sustaining.

My own understanding of this took shape one winter morning. I was reviewing my long-term plan as the early light came through the window. Outside was cold and still, and the quiet gave me space to think. I had built a career over decades, but as I reviewed each source of future income, I realized something important. The goal was not to maximize any single stream. The goal was to design a sequence. A structure. A progression across time where each layer would appear when needed and recede when not. Income stacking was not about accumulation. It was about choreography.

That morning reshaped how I thought about the second half of life. It made me see income not as a number but as a timeline. A set of arrivals. A set of transitions that would unfold naturally if I designed them well.

The first layer is work, but it does not last forever. The next layers matter more because they represent continuity, stability, and time. They are the incomes that arrive even when you are not working. They are the incomes that strengthen your future self. They form a sequence that carries you from one stage of life to the next.

For some people, the first durable layer is a pension or pension-like annuity. It is simple, predictable, and steady. It does not require management or attention. It arrives reliably. A pension is not glamorous, but it is one of the purest forms of income stability a person can have.

The second layer could be rental income. It can be modest or substantial, but what matters is not the amount. It is the durability. Rental income is consistent. It does not move with the daily rhythm of markets. It rewards long-term care and design. It offers inflation protection. It adds ballast. But this layer only compounds if it is built to be stress-light rather than management-heavy—where careful tenant selection, sensible leverage, and disciplined attention to after-tax yield ensure the income remains durable and net positive after fees, maintenance, and inevitable friction.

The third layer is dividends and interest. These come from ownership. They come from a lifetime of disciplined investing. They do not feel like much in the early years, but they grow, and then they grow faster, and eventually they form a meaningful stream that arrives without prompting. These streams are the quiet confirmation that compounding is at work.

The fourth layer is income drawn from both taxable and tax-advantaged accounts: brokerage accounts, 401(k)s, IRAs, and Roth IRAs. This is not just income. It is freedom. It is the ability to draw from a pool of money that preserves flexibility in your future tax position. It is one of the rare gifts that rewards patience with complete flexibility later in life.

The fifth layer is Social Security. It is often underestimated, but it represents longevity insurance. It is a stabilizer. It is a base that arrives every month, regardless of markets or economic cycles, and is adjusted for inflation each year. When delayed until later in life, it becomes an anchor.

These layers do not need to be perfect. They do not need to be optimized. They simply need to exist. Once they are in place, they support you in ways that a single stream of income never could.

What makes income stacking so powerful is not just the presence of multiple streams, but the way they interact under stress. A single source of income can feel sufficient when conditions are favorable. But life is rarely linear. Careers pause or end unexpectedly. Markets experience long periods of volatility. Health shifts. Priorities change. Income stacking is the quiet discipline of designing for those moments in advance, rather than reacting to them when they arrive.

When income is layered thoughtfully, pressure dissipates. No single stream carries the full burden of supporting your life. Work can be reduced without fear. Markets can fluctuate without panic. Decisions can be made from a position of stability rather than urgency. This is the difference between having income and having resilience.

Resilience, in this context, is not about abundance. It is about redundancy. The presence of overlapping sources that step in when another recedes. Work income eventually fades. That is expected. But pensions, rental income, dividends, and structured withdrawals do not all arrive or decline at the same time. Their staggered nature is not accidental. It is the feature that makes the system durable.

This is why income stacking should be designed conservatively. Not optimized for maximum yield, but for reliability and ease. Income that arrives predictably often does more for your life than income that arrives dramatically but unpredictably. The goal is not to impress a spreadsheet. The goal is to create a structure you can live inside comfortably for decades.

One of the most underappreciated aspects of income stacking is the way it changes your relationship with time. When income is diversified across stages of life, urgency loosens its grip. You are no longer forced to extract maximum value from every working year. You can choose when to slow down. You can step away from roles that no longer fit. You can reallocate your attention toward health, relationships, and meaning without destabilizing your financial foundation.

This flexibility becomes increasingly valuable as life grows more complex. In midlife, income stacking creates room for recalibration. It allows you to adjust course without disruption. In later life, it simplifies decision-making. You are no longer solving for income each year. You are stewarding a system that already knows what to do.

Importantly, income stacking is not about building everything at once. Each layer arrives through its own season. Trying to force them simultaneously often leads to unnecessary strain. The long game respects timing. It allows work to dominate early. It lets ownership compound in the background. It introduces durability gradually. And it delays irreversible decisions until clarity is high and pressure is low.

There is also a psychological benefit to income stacking that is rarely discussed. When income is diversified, identity loosens its attachment to any single role. You are not only what you earn today. You are supported by what you built yesterday and what you designed for tomorrow. This shift creates calm. It reduces the emotional weight of career decisions. It allows you to engage with work as a choice rather than a necessity.

Income stacking turns effort into optionality. It converts

decades of discipline into daily freedom. It allows your financial life to recede into the background where it belongs, doing its job while you focus on living well.

In the end, income stacking is not a strategy for maximizing wealth. It is a strategy for minimizing fragility. It transforms income from something you chase into something that arrives. It replaces dependence with design. And it ensures that as life evolves, your financial foundation evolves with it, steady, supportive, and largely out of view.

Income stacking is not about maximizing every source at once. It is about sequencing. Different forms of income become useful at different stages of life, overlapping just enough to reduce fragility while preserving flexibility. The figure illustrates when each source typically becomes relevant, not when it must begin. Actual timing of each source will vary—the graph is for illustrative purposes only. More in the Appendix.

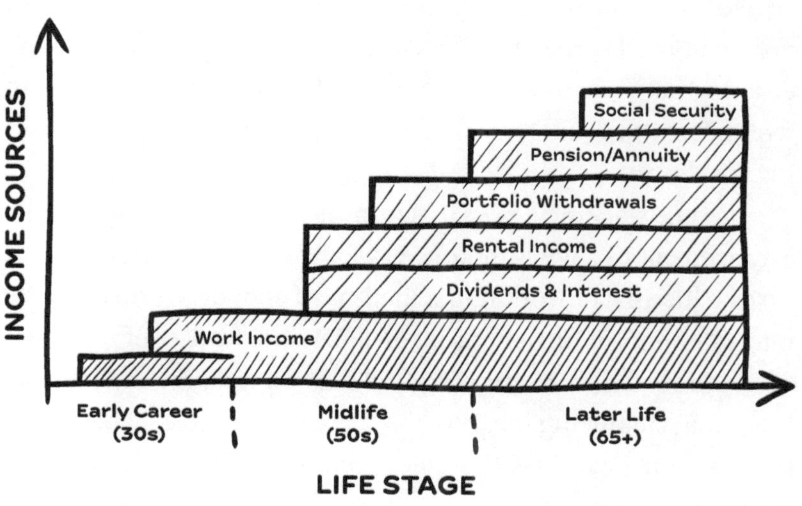

FIGURE 7 The Architecture of Lifetime Income

For someone in their twenties, income stacking begins with one idea: Build assets that work while you sleep. It does not matter if the amounts are small. What matters is the direction. Own broad market funds, preferably the S&P 500. Contribute consistently. Build skills that increase your earning potential. Keep your expenses low enough that early investments have room to compound. Income stacking at this stage is not about diversification. It is about planting seeds.

For someone in midlife, income stacking becomes a strategic exercise. It is where decisions carry long-term weight. You shift from building assets to shaping how those assets will sustain you. You reduce fragility by widening your sources of income. You prepare for future transitions instead of reacting to them. You begin to design the order of operations that will carry you into the next decades. Pension or annuity income, rental income, dividends, interest, tax-advantaged withdrawals, and eventually Social Security all become part of a larger rhythm.

For someone later in life, income stacking becomes a plan of preservation. It protects independence. It simplifies decisions. It ensures that your lifestyle is supported by structure rather than stress. It shifts your attention from building wealth to maintaining freedom.

Income stacking across a lifetime is not complicated. It is the arrangement of a few simple layers. But simplicity is powerful. It turns a lifetime of work into a lifetime of support. It turns assets into autonomy. It turns decades of effort into decades of meaning.

In the end, income stacking is not about maximizing income. It is about stabilizing life. It is about creating a future where your time is your own. It is the quiet architecture of a life designed with care.

CHAPTER 13

The Art of Lifetime Tax Design

Taxes shape the slope of your financial life far more than most people ever notice.

Most people think of taxes as a yearly obligation. Something to complete. Something to minimize. Something that arrives in the spring and disappears again. But taxes, when viewed across a lifetime, are not a seasonal inconvenience. They are a structural force. They determine how much of your compounding you keep and how much you surrender. Taxes influence the slope of your financial life more than investment returns, market predictions, or opinions about the economy.

The tax strategies that matter most are not complicated. They are not clever. They do not require specialized knowledge. They reward patience, timing, and long-term behavior. When understood correctly, they change the shape of a life.

I first understood this during a quiet evening at home. I was sitting in my study, reviewing a financial projection that stretched decades ahead. I traced the flow of future income, the timing of pensions, the balance between taxable and tax-advantaged accounts, and the eventual role of Social Security. As the projection came into focus, something became clear. The most powerful lever across those decades was not market performance. It was sequencing. The order in which income appears. The tax treatment of each withdrawal. The design choices made long before the money ever arrives.

Once you see taxes as a lifelong sequence rather than a yearly task, your entire approach changes.

What most people never see is the cost of ignoring this sequencing. It does not arrive as a bill or a penalty. It shows up years later, in the form of lost flexibility. Money that could have been drawn tax-free becomes taxable. Income that could have been smoothed arrives in spikes. Decisions that could have been optional become forced. Nothing catastrophic happens. But something subtle is lost—control.

This is why lifetime tax design matters even for people who do everything else "right." You can save diligently, invest wisely, avoid debt, and still give away far more than necessary simply by failing to think across time. The danger is not ignorance. It is default. Taxes are one of the few forces in life that will happily take whatever you do not intentionally protect.

The most common pattern looks like this. During high-earning years, people defer aggressively into pre-tax accounts, understandably grateful for the immediate deduction. They assume they will "deal with taxes later," when income is lower. Then life unfolds. Work ends. Pensions begin. Social Security starts. Required minimum distributions arrive. Income does not fall the way it was imagined. In some cases, it rises. What once felt like a tax deferral reveals itself as a tax concentration.

By then, options are limited. Large balances create large, forced withdrawals. The window for strategic conversion has closed. Taxes become something to manage rather than something to design. The opportunity was never missed in a single year. It was missed across many quiet ones.

The irony is that the years with the most leverage are often the least celebrated. The early retirement years. The gap between full-time work and full-time income. The years when life feels lighter and the calendar opens up. These are the years when thoughtful tax design does its best work. Income is lower. Brackets are available. Decisions can be made calmly rather than reactively.

This is also where temperament matters. Lifetime tax planning requires patience. It asks you to pay some tax earlier than feels strictly necessary in order to reduce uncertainty later. It rewards the ability to think in trade-offs rather than absolutes. It favors people who are willing to accept a known cost today to avoid an unknown one tomorrow.

What makes this challenging is that good tax decisions rarely feel urgent. There is no flashing signal telling you to act. The penalty for waiting is not immediate. But time, once passed, does not return. Brackets close. Options narrow. Flexibility erodes. The long game shifts against you.

A well-designed tax strategy does something powerful. It smooths your financial life. It reduces spikes. It protects against regret. It allows you to move through different stages of life without constantly renegotiating your relationship with money. It gives you agency when circumstances change.

Just as important, it gives you peace. You no longer wonder if you should have done something earlier. You are not forced into last-minute decisions. You are not reacting to rules you did not design. You are operating from a position of foresight rather than cleanup.

This is why lifetime tax design belongs alongside portfolio design, income stacking, and stewardship. It is not an optimization exercise. It is an alignment exercise. It ensures that the wealth you have built continues to serve you rather than surprise you. It allows compounding to work not just in markets, but in clarity.

In the end, the goal is not to eliminate taxes. That is neither realistic nor necessary. The goal is to retain agency. To decide when and how income arrives. To keep more of what you have earned not by cleverness, but by sequence. When you approach taxes this way, they stop being an annual annoyance and become part of a life designed with intention.

That is the quiet power of lifetime tax design. It is not about eliminating taxes, but about choosing *when* you pay them, and doing so deliberately rather than by default.

The logic behind this is straightforward. Taxes rise when

income rises and fall when income falls. Yet most people focus only on minimizing taxes this year, missing the far more important opportunity to minimize taxes across all years. The years that matter most are the quiet ones. The transitions. The early retirement period between full-time work and the onset of pensions or Social Security. These years create a window that many never recognize: a Roth conversion window—the first principle.

A Roth conversion allows you to move money from a pre-tax account into a Roth account, paying taxes today so your future self can withdraw the funds tax-free. The mistake most people make is assuming conversions should happen during high-income years or only when markets decline. In reality, the best time to convert is during low-income years, particularly the early years of retirement when work income has stopped but pensions and Social Security have not yet begun. These years allow you to fill the lower tax brackets intentionally. You convert up to the top of a bracket, such as the 24 percent bracket, without spilling into the next one. You use the space deliberately. You smooth the tax burden of future decades. You prevent large required minimum distributions (RMDs) later in life. And you ensure that more of your compounding stays with you rather than flowing to taxes.

The second principle is that tax planning is not about prediction. It is about protection. You do not need to know what future tax rates will be. You need to build optionality. A balanced structure of taxable, pre-tax, and Roth accounts gives you the flexibility to choose the most efficient withdrawal source each year. Flexibility is one of the greatest financial advantages a person can have. In tax planning, optionality is worth more than precision.

The third principle is that the most damaging tax mistakes

often happen late. Large pre-tax balances can create forced withdrawals that push income into high brackets. Required minimum distributions (RMDs) can create tax spikes at precisely the wrong time. Markets can move in ways that complicate reactive decisions. Early planning solves all three. It prevents the need for urgency. It widens the margin for error. It protects your future self from the unintended consequences of inaction.

For someone in their twenties, the tax strategy that matters most is simple. Contribute consistently. Favor Roth accounts and tax-advantaged accounts, such as a 401(k), while your income is modest. Build habits that will serve you decades later. At this stage, momentum outweighs optimization.

For someone in midlife, the tax strategy becomes intentional sequencing. It is the period where income peaks, responsibilities widen, and the future begins to take shape. This is where you design the order in which your accounts will eventually support your life. It is where you plan your Roth conversion window, allowing you to reduce future required minimum distributions (RMDs) and retain greater control later in life. It is where clarity becomes more important than complexity.

For someone later in life, the tax strategy becomes a form of preservation. It protects independence. It minimizes forced decisions. It ensures that wealth transitions smoothly. It simplifies the years when stability matters more than accumulation.

The quiet truth is that tax planning is not a technical exercise. It is a behavioral one. It rewards foresight. It rewards calm. It rewards the person willing to think in decades rather than years. The person who views their financial life as a sequence rather than a collection of disconnected events.

A lifetime tax strategy is ultimately about one thing. It is about strengthening your future self. It is about retaining more of what you have built. It is about designing a financial life that compounds smoothly rather than reactively.

When viewed in this way, tax planning becomes something deeper than efficiency. It becomes stewardship. It becomes care. It becomes one of the most powerful advantages in the long game.

CHAPTER 14
Money as Fuel, Not Identity

Wealth is fuel for a life well lived,
not proof of one.

There is a point in every financial life when money begins to take on meaning beyond numbers. In the early years, it represents possibility. Later, it can become a source of security. Eventually, for many people, it evolves into something else entirely. It becomes identity. It becomes the metric through which they interpret their progress, their value, and their place in the world.

This shift often happens gradually, not through intention but through drift. And left unexamined, it becomes one of the most costly transitions in a person's life. Not costly financially, but costly in clarity, direction, and peace.

Money is not meant to be identity. It is meant to be fuel. Fuel for autonomy. Fuel for exploration. Fuel for a life that compounds. When money becomes identity instead of fuel, the entire system breaks.

I saw this clearly one evening while reviewing old journals and decisions I had made across different stages of life. The entries and themes from my early twenties were simple. I was focused on learning, saving, and building a margin around my life. The entries from my thirties were about responsibility and growth. But somewhere in the middle years, the tone shifted. The decisions were still rational, but the motivation behind them was more complex. The stakes felt higher. The wins and losses meant more than they should have. That evening, I realized something important. I had allowed parts of my identity to merge with financial performance. It happened subtly, without intention, but it happened.

Recognizing this changed everything. Money needed to return to its proper role in my life. It needed to become fuel again.

What I came to see is that this shift rarely happens through conscious choice. There is a subtle psychological shift that occurs when money becomes abundant enough to stop being purely instrumental. In the early years, money is clearly a means. It solves obvious problems. It creates safety. It expands possibility. But once basic needs are met and future security feels plausible, money begins to change its role. It starts to invite comparison. It becomes a scoreboard. And without careful attention, it begins to measure worth rather than support life.

This is where many people lose their footing.

When money becomes identity, decisions stop being guided by values and start being guided by preservation of status. Risk tolerance becomes distorted. Spending becomes performative. Saving becomes defensive. Even generosity can become transactional. The inner posture shifts from stewardship to self-protection. Life narrows, not because resources are scarce, but because meaning has been outsourced to metrics.

The cost of this shift is not immediately visible. Externally, life may appear successful. Internally, however, tension grows. Wins no longer satisfy. Losses feel personal. Comparison creeps into places where it never belonged. Financial outcomes begin to carry emotional weight they were never designed to bear. The mind becomes preoccupied with maintaining an image rather than building a life.

This is why money must remain fuel.

Fuel is neutral. It has purpose, not meaning. It is valuable precisely because it enables motion without defining direction. When money is treated as fuel, it supports choices without dictating them. It gives energy to what matters rather than replacing it. It allows ambition without attachment and success without fragility.

One of the quiet disciplines of the long game is repeatedly returning money to this role.

This does not mean disengagement from wealth. It means re-anchoring it. It means asking better questions. Does this decision expand my future or narrow it? Does it create optionality or obligation? Does it protect my time, my health, and my attention, or does it gradually consume them? These questions restore proportion. They keep money aligned with purpose rather than ego.

As life progresses, this discipline becomes more important, not less. The more financial capacity you have, the greater the risk that money begins to shape identity by default. Titles fade. Roles change. Careers evolve or end. If worth has been tied too closely to financial output, these transitions can feel destabilizing. But when money has remained fuel, transition becomes lighter. The structure remains intact even as the surface changes.

This posture also changes how success is defined. Wealth is no longer measured by accumulation alone, but by the quality of life it enables. Freedom of movement. Freedom of time. Freedom from unnecessary stress. Freedom to choose depth over display. These forms of wealth are quiet, but they endure.

There is a calm confidence that comes from this alignment. It does not need reinforcement. It does not seek validation. It allows you to enjoy what you have without being owned by it. Money does its job, and then it recedes into the background where it belongs.

The long game rewards this restraint. When money remains fuel, it compounds in service of a life that feels expansive rather than performative. It supports vitality instead of competing with it. It protects meaning rather than replacing it. And it allows wealth to mature into something rarer than success: sufficiency paired with clarity.

This is not a renunciation of ambition. It is its refinement. It is the recognition that money is most powerful when it enables identity, not when it becomes one.

For someone early in their career, the danger is lifestyle creep. Income rises, and so do expectations. The gap between earnings and spending narrows until there is no margin left to invest. The trap is that lifestyle becomes a quiet identity builder. Dining out regularly. Upgraded homes. Designer purchases. None of these are wrong, but they can become anchors that weigh down freedom. The antidote is simple. Treat money as fuel for your long game. Build tax literacy early. Learn to live just slightly below your rising means so your future expands rather than contracts. Develop the discipline to invest consistently. A quiet, simple life early on becomes a powerful life later.

In midlife, the danger is different. It is identity loss. Many people spend decades building careers that become intertwined with who they believe themselves to be. Their net worth, their titles, their earning power. When this identity meets transition, whether voluntary or not, the disorientation can be profound. Here, the challenge is not to resist ambition or achievement. It is to avoid confusing external markers with internal worth. Money is not meant to define you. It is meant to support the next chapter of your life, not imprison you inside the current one.

Real wealth is quiet. It does not need to be expressed. It does not chase validation. It does not require recognition. It operates beneath the surface. It creates room to think, space to breathe, and the freedom to make decisions aligned with who you are becoming. A stoic form of wealth understands that the point is not accumulation for its own sake. It is the creation of optionality, autonomy, and clarity.

Money, when treated as fuel, gives you the ability to make better decisions. It gives you the power to say no. It protects your time and energy. It supports your future self in ways that expand your life rather than confine it. But when money becomes identity, it narrows your world. It ties your worth to outcomes you cannot fully control. It creates anxiety where there should be clarity.

The long game is not about wealth. It is about freedom. It is about designing a life where money supports your deepest values and experiences instead of overshadowing them. It is about maintaining the posture that financial success should enlarge your character, not replace it.

Life is a balanced fund with three core assets: Capital, Vitality, and Time. Capital compounds financially. Vitality compounds biologically. Time compounds existentially. The more of it you have, the more wisely you can reinvest it. Ultimately, prioritizing Health ROI over Financial ROI is a declaration of independence, not from work, but from the illusion that income equals more life. Once financial sufficiency is reached, money stops buying freedom and starts buying maintenance. Health, when cultivated deliberately, buys time that feels expansive.

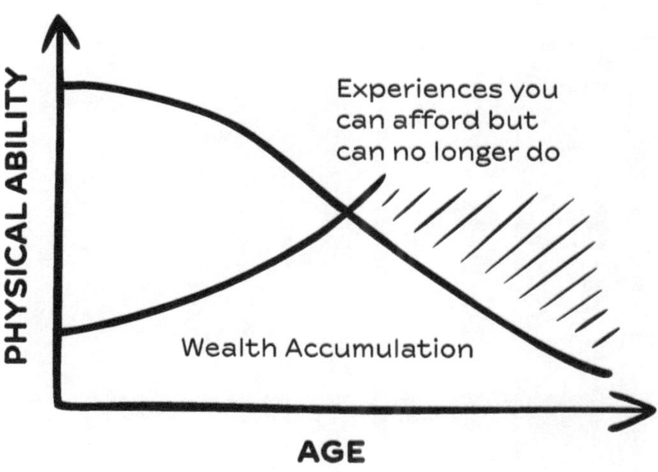

FIGURE 8 The Quiet Arbitrage Between Health and Wealth
When financial capacity outpaces physical ability, the range of life begins to narrow. As wealth compounds later in life, physical ability often declines, creating a widening gap between what we can afford and what we can still fully do. These are the experiences we postponed, assuming time would always be available, only to discover that money arrived after capacity had already begun to fade.

This is the quiet arbitrage between health and wealth. When health compounds early, wealth expands what is possible. When health is neglected, wealth arrives too late to fully redeem time.

When money returns to its role as fuel, everything becomes lighter. Decisions become clearer. Perspective widens. You begin to see that the real measure of wealth is not what you accumulate, but the life it allows you to build and experience. Wealth is the foundation that lets you pursue meaning without compromise. It is the tool that protects your future self. It is the structure that gives you room to evolve.

Money as fuel is the essence of quiet wealth and the antidote to identity-based wealth. It is the mindset that allows the next phases of your life to unfold with clarity. And it is one of the most important transitions in the long game.

PART III

VITALITY

*The Body as the Chassis
of The Long Game*

CHAPTER 15

The Longevity Mindset

*Longevity is not about extending life.
It is about protecting the freedom
to live it fully.*

At some level, we all eventually realize that health is not about performance. It is about capacity. It is about the physical freedom to move through your days with strength, clarity, and presence. It is about having a body that supports the life you want rather than limits it. Some people learn this early. Many learn it late. But eventually, everyone learns it. The body sets the boundaries. vitality widens them.

A longevity mindset begins with accepting a simple truth. The body you build is the life you get to live. Not in a superficial way. Not in the pursuit of aesthetics or quick fixes. But in the quiet, structural sense. The body is the chassis for decades of decisions. It determines your resilience, your confidence, and your capacity to play the long game. When you understand this, health stops being a project and becomes a philosophy.

And like most philosophical errors, the cost of ignoring longevity is rarely dramatic. It is quieter. It is the gradual narrowing of possibility.

Most physical decline does not arrive as a crisis. It arrives as a series of small accommodations. You stop taking the stairs. You choose closer parking. You hesitate before committing to trips that require long walks, uneven terrain, or long days. You recover more slowly, so you plan less. You protect energy instead of expanding it. None of these moments feel decisive. But together, they redraw the map of your life.

This is how vitality is lost. Not through catastrophe, but through constraint.

The cruel irony is that many people reach their highest levels of financial and intellectual freedom just as their physical capacity begins to erode. They finally have the time, resources, and autonomy to travel, explore, learn, and create—yet their bodies veto the opportunities. Experiences remain affordable but no longer accessible. Freedom exists on paper, not in practice.

This is the quiet arbitrage most people miss.

A longevity mindset closes that gap. It ensures that physical capacity keeps pace with financial and intellectual growth. It treats health as infrastructure rather than insurance. The work is not glamorous, but the payoff is profound. Every year of consistent training preserves optionality. Every decade compounds it.

Without this mindset, health becomes reactive. You train when something hurts. You change habits when a warning light appears. You outsource responsibility to specialists instead of owning the system. The result is fragility. Not dramatic weakness, but a body that requires constant negotiation.

With a longevity mindset, the posture reverses. Training becomes preventive rather than corrective. Recovery becomes intentional rather than accidental. Strength, endurance, and mobility are maintained as baseline capabilities, not emergency responses. The body becomes reliable.

This reliability changes how you move through the world.

You make plans with confidence instead of contingency. You say yes without calculating recovery time. You invest in experiences knowing your body can support them. This creates a subtle but powerful psychological shift. You begin to trust yourself again—not just intellectually, but physically.

This trust compounds.

A strong, capable body reduces cognitive load. Decisions feel easier when fatigue is lower. Stress is metabolized through movement rather than stored. Sleep deepens. Mood stabilizes. The mental clarity people search for through productivity systems often emerges naturally when physical capacity is restored.

The long game demands endurance. Not just cardiovascular endurance, but existential endurance. The ability to stay engaged with life across decades. The ability to remain curious, energetic, and physically present long after novelty fades.

Longevity is not about adding years to life. It is about protecting life inside the years.

When you adopt this mindset, training stops competing with your ambitions and begins supporting them. Health no longer feels like maintenance. It feels like leverage. You are no longer preparing for decline. You are preparing for continuity.

The consequence of this mindset is not visible in a mirror or a metric. It is visible in the breadth of your life. In how long you remain capable. In how fully you inhabit the freedom you worked so hard to build.

This is why vitality belongs alongside capital and intellect in the long game. Without it, the system is incomplete. With it, everything else compounds more smoothly.

My understanding of this did not emerge overnight. It began decades ago, long before I ever thought seriously about longevity. I was an NCAA student-athlete in college, training daily, thinking of my body as something nearly inexhaustible. Back then, strength and endurance were simply part of life. I never questioned whether I could bounce back or push harder. I never wondered if I would have the capacity to do what I wanted. Youth disguised effort as inevitability.

But years later, the reality became clear. The physical foundation I had taken for granted in my twenties had eroded slowly in the background of a demanding career, long flights, stress, and responsibility. What remained was memory more than capability. The athletic identity had faded, but the desire for physical competence had not. That tension became a catalyst for change.

The moment it crystallized was quiet. I was in my home study, the place where I think through long-term plans and the shape of my future. I pulled up my training data from Garmin and saw the story it was telling. Strength returning. Endurance rising. VO_2 max climbing. Recovery improving. It wasn't nostalgia. It wasn't a desire to be who I was in college. It was the recognition that I could build a body for the next thirty years of my life, not the last thirty.

A longevity mindset has nothing to do with age. It is about orientation. It is about replacing short-term goals with long-term architecture. It is the rejection of the belief that youth determines vitality. It is the acceptance that discipline, consistency, and intelligent training can rebuild the body at any stage.

For a twenty-something, this mindset is an unmatched advantage. Most people coast on youth without realizing how quickly the years pass. Strength fades. Endurance declines. Mobility narrows. But small habits built early compound more than any investment. Regular strength training. Sustainable cardiovascular work. A simple nutrition philosophy. A consistent sleep rhythm. These habits build a body that will serve you for decades. They create optionality. They reduce future volatility. They spare you from the painful work of rebuilding what you allowed to erode.

For someone in midlife, the longevity mindset becomes a competitive advantage. It is the moment when health is no longer abstract. It is visceral. You can feel the difference between strong and weak. Between energetic and depleted. Between being the driver of your life and being a passenger. This season of life is not a decline. It is a leverage point. Strength can return. Endurance can surpass earlier baselines. Mobility can be restored. Body composition can change in profound ways. With intelligence and consistency, you can outperform younger versions of yourself.

The longevity mindset begins with three core ideas.

The first is **ownership**. No one else is coming to save your health. Not a doctor. Not a program. Not a supplement. Health is built through daily choices. Those choices compound. They either expand your life or shrink it.

The second is **capability**. Longevity is not about looking fit. It is about being capable. It is about being able to carry weight. Move quickly. Climb stairs. Cycle for hours. Hike for miles with load. Ski with control while fatigued. Recover overnight. Use your body the way life requires. Capability is the currency of vitality.

The third is **identity**. You do not become fit because you hope to. You become fit because you see yourself as someone who trains with purpose. Someone who honors their future self. Someone who treats their body as an asset rather than an afterthought. When identity shifts, behavior follows.

A longevity mindset is not about reaching a peak. It is about extending the slope. It is about building a body that does not betray you. It is about creating a life where you can travel, explore, lift, cycle, ruck, ski, hike, think, and create well into your later decades. Health becomes a form of freedom. Strength becomes a form of confidence. Endurance becomes a form of resilience.

Most people underestimate what is possible in a year. Almost everyone underestimates what is possible in a decade. Your body is not fixed. It is malleable. It responds to attention, intention, and consistency. When you adopt a longevity mindset, you stop negotiating with your health. You stop postponing the work you know you need to do. You stop thinking in terms of seasons and start thinking in terms of decades.

The longevity mindset is not about becoming exceptional. It is about becoming durable. It is about creating a life where your physical capacity amplifies your intellectual and financial life. It is the recognition that health is not separate from success. It is the infrastructure that makes success possible.

This is the beginning of vitality. The quiet power that shapes the next chapters of your life. The foundation upon which everything else rests.

CHAPTER 16

VO$_2$ Max: The New Wealth Index

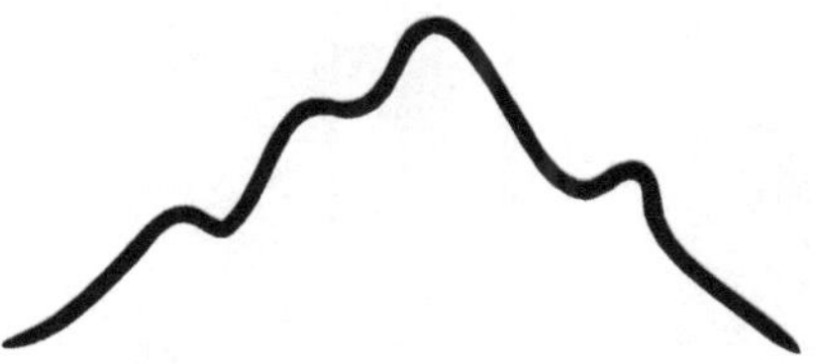

A larger engine does not just extend life.
It expands it.

There is a simple truth about health that most people do not discover until they need it. Strength matters. Nutrition matters. Sleep matters. Among all measurable markers of vitality, cardiorespiratory fitness stands near the top. VO_2 max, your maximal ability to take in, transport, and utilize oxygen, is one of its clearest expressions. It is one of the strongest single physiological predictors we have for longevity and functional independence. Higher levels of aerobic capacity are consistently associated with lower risk of all-cause mortality, often rivaling or exceeding traditional risk factors such as hypertension, hyperlipidemia, and smoking. In that sense, aerobic capacity functions as a modern wealth index, a quiet measure of how much margin your body carries into the decades ahead.

The idea is straightforward. A higher VO_2 max means a larger engine. A larger engine means a more resilient body. A more resilient body means more years, more capability, and more freedom. It means a life shaped by possibility rather than limitation.

What makes VO_2 max so powerful is not that it predicts performance. It predicts margin. It is the difference between moving through life with ease and negotiating every physical demand.

Most people assume decline announces itself dramatically. In reality, it arrives gradually, through small accommodations that accumulate. You plan your days more carefully. You choose convenience over curiosity. You recover more slowly, so you hesitate before committing. Travel feels heavier. Long walks feel optional. Stairs become something to avoid rather than ignore. None of these moments feel decisive. Together, they redraw the boundaries of your life.

That realization changed how I approached my own health. I wanted a number that reflected capacity, not perception.

I began tracking my fitness age through objective markers: VO_2 max, resting heart rate, recovery trends. The data were eye-opening. They revealed how easily effort can feel sufficient while capacity remains unchanged. Measuring health not by the absence of illness, but by the margin I was building for decades ahead, changed how I thought about my future.

Fitness, like capital, compounds only when tracked and tended. The goal is not perfection. It is consistency. Metrics do not replace judgment, but they prevent self-deception.

True VO_2 max is a laboratory measure of oxygen uptake, and large outcome studies assess cardiorespiratory fitness more broadly than the algorithmic estimates produced by consumer devices. The distinction matters. Capacity is real. Device readings are approximations.

In a large 2018 study of more than 120,000 adults undergoing treadmill testing, higher cardiorespiratory fitness, measured in metabolic equivalents (METs), was strongly and independently associated with lower all-cause mortality.[6]

A strong aerobic engine gives you slack in the system. It allows you to absorb stress without breaking rhythm. Recovery accelerates. The engine becomes predictable. You are not constantly budgeting effort. You simply move.

When VO_2 max erodes, the opposite happens. Every demand carries a cost. Decisions become filtered through fatigue. Life narrows not because you choose less, but because the body limits what feels reasonable.

This narrowing often happens during the busiest and most productive years of life. Careers peak. Responsibilities expand. Travel increases. Stress compounds. Movement declines. Aerobic fitness slips below the threshold needed to support the life you are building. And because the decline is gradual, it goes unnoticed until capacity is already compromised.

What makes this especially dangerous is that VO_2 max does not announce its loss with pain. You can feel functional while becoming fragile. You can look healthy while losing resilience. This is why many people confuse "fine" with fit, and why the consequences arrive later than the choices that created them.

VO_2 max is not just a health metric. It is a form of insurance. It protects your future self from the compounding effects of inactivity, stress, and time. It preserves the ability to say yes without calculation. Yes to long days. Yes to unfamiliar terrain. Yes to effort without hesitation.

There is also an asymmetry worth understanding. Losing aerobic capacity is easy. Rebuilding it later is costly. Not impossible but demanding. It requires intention, structure, and patience. The earlier you protect it, the less work it takes to maintain. The longer you neglect it, the steeper the climb back becomes.

This is why VO_2 max deserves to be treated like a balance sheet item. Not something you optimize once, but something you monitor, protect, and deliberately grow. It compounds like capital. Small gains, sustained over a lifetime, produce outsized returns in later decades. And like capital, neglect leads to erosion that is far harder to reverse than it was to prevent.

A high VO_2 max does not guarantee longevity. But a low one reliably predicts fragility. It increases vulnerability to illness, injury, and fatigue. It shrinks the buffer between stress and breakdown. It turns ordinary life into something that requires recovery rather than something that generates energy.

The long game demands more than survival. It demands capacity. The capacity to think clearly under pressure. To travel without exhaustion. To train without injury. To explore without fear of recovery. To live fully in the decades you worked to reach.

This is the deeper reason VO₂ max belongs in a conversation about wealth. Not because it can be measured. But because it determines how much of your wealth you can actually use. A strong engine allows you to spend your time, money, and attention freely. A weak one forces tradeoffs long before you expect them.

VO₂ max is the quiet arbiter of freedom. It does not shout. It does not impress. But it decides how wide your world remains.

My relationship with VO₂ max was not always intentional. For many years, it sat in the background of my athletic life without being named. In my twenties, training daily as a student-athlete, I never thought about oxygen uptake or cardiac output. I simply trained hard, recovered quickly, and took for granted the engine I had built through repetition, conditioning, and youth. But as the years passed and my career accelerated, the quiet erosion began. Flights. Meetings. Stress. Less movement. The engine was still there, but its output had dulled.

Years later, when I recommitted to rebuilding my physical foundation, VO₂ max became more than a metric. It became a compass. And the first meaningful progress did not come from interval training or structured programming. It came from cycling.

Cycling has always been one of the purest forms of endurance. I began riding regularly in my forties through Bucks County, Pennsylvania, weaving along rolling roads framed by farmland, tree-lined climbs, and long, quiet stretches that allowed me to settle into a rhythm. These rides were not about speed. They were about building a Zone 2 base, the aerobic foundation that underlies almost every marker of long-term cardiovascular health. The terrain itself became a teacher. The gentle slopes sustained my Zone 2 cadence. The steeper hills nudged me toward threshold work without forcing maximal effort. Ride after ride, my engine began to wake up again.

There was a morning on a familiar Bucks County loop when I realized something was changing. The hills felt less imposing. My breathing stayed even. My legs recovered more quickly. My heart rate stabilized faster at the top of each climb. The data would confirm it later, but the sensation came first. Cycling was rebuilding my capacity from the inside out.

As my conditioning returned, I added something more targeted. The Norwegian 4×4 protocol. Four minutes of high effort. Three minutes of recovery. Repeated four times. Simple. Demanding. Highly effective. The first sessions were uncomfortable. The heart rate climbed quickly. The recovery windows felt short. But the impact was undeniable. My VO₂ max began to rise in a way that cycling alone had not achieved. The 4×4s pushed the ceiling. The riding built the floor. Together, they created the most powerful combination I had encountered for improving cardiorespiratory fitness.

Tracking all of this through my Garmin dashboard became a form of intelligence gathering. It gave me an honest reflection of recovery, sleep, strain, and adaptation. I could see the cumulative effect of the rides, the intervals, the rest days, and even the quiet patterns of daily life. The data did not control my training. It guided it. It allowed me to see progress long before it was visible in the mirror.

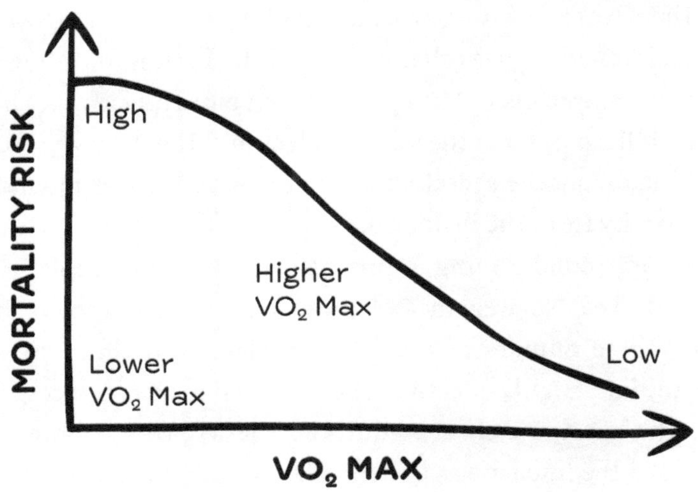

FIGURE 9 The Capacity Curve
This curve illustrates one of the most consistent findings in longevity science: the more capacity you build, the lower your mortality risk. Data from a large 2018 *JAMA* study of more than 120,000 adults showed a clear, graded relationship between cardiorespiratory fitness and all-cause mortality. Moving from "below average" to "above average" fitness sharply reduced risk, and the highest-fitness group (the top 2.5%) experienced the lowest mortality of all, with benefits comparable to or greater than eliminating major risk factors.[6] Expanded in the Appendix.

In practical terms, increasing your VO_2 max is one of the most reliable levers you control for extending both lifespan and healthspan. Even modest improvements shift you onto a healthier trajectory and widen the number of years in which you remain strong, capable, and independent.

For someone in their twenties, building a strong VO_2 max is one of the greatest long-term advantages available. Youth amplifies adaptation. Training compounds quickly. Small habits create an engine that can carry you for decades. This is the season when endurance is easiest to build and easiest to protect. Establishing a baseline early sets the trajectory for the decades that follow.

For someone in their fifties, VO_2 max becomes something else. It becomes evidence that decline is not inevitable. It becomes proof that physiology responds to intention, not just age. Many people assume their best days of fitness are behind them. Yet the science is clear. VO_2 max can rise at any age. It can improve dramatically with structure and consistency. You can, in a very real sense, grow younger from the inside out.

In the end, VO_2 max is not about performance. It is about freedom. It is about the ability to cycle for hours. Ruck for miles. Hike without limitation. Travel without fatigue. Live without physical compromise. It is the measure that determines how fully you can experience the decades ahead.

A strong engine extends your slope. It protects your autonomy. It expands your life. It is the new wealth index for a long and meaningful life.

CHAPTER 17
The Tier 1 Civilian Protocol

Durability is capacity extended across time.

There is a particular kind of strength that does not come from specialization. It comes from capability. It comes from being able to move through the world with confidence, resilience, and physical readiness. It is the strength required to live a long, capable life. A life where your body is an asset, not a liability. A life where you are prepared for more than the gym. You are prepared for the terrain of life itself.

This is the idea behind the Tier 1 Civilian Protocol. It is not a workout plan. It is not a program. It is a philosophy for building a durable body. It is a framework for ordinary people who want extraordinary longevity. It is the disciplined middle ground between elite performance and quiet, sustainable fitness. It is a protocol for a life measured in decades.

Seen through that lens, the greatest misunderstanding about fitness is that it is about improvement. In reality, it is about preservation. Most people do not lose their physical capacity in a dramatic collapse. They lose it slowly, through neglect, specialization, and misplaced priorities. They become efficient at a narrow slice of life while becoming fragile everywhere else.

Modern fitness culture amplifies this mistake. It rewards aesthetics over function. Specialization over capability. Short-term transformation over long-term resilience. You can be strong but brittle. Lean but exhausted. Fit for the gym but unprepared for real terrain. This is how people end up surprised by injury, decline, or limitation. Not because they were inactive, but because they trained without a framework.

The real threat is not inactivity. It is imbalance.

A body trained only for appearance loses strength where it matters most. A body trained only for endurance loses muscle and structural integrity. A body trained without mobility accumulates restriction and compensation. A body trained without a core becomes unstable under load. Each omission compounds until something fails.

This is where the idea of a protocol matters.

A protocol is different from a routine. A routine is what you do. A protocol is why it works. A routine can be followed blindly. A protocol adapts. It governs decisions. It provides guardrails. It ensures that effort compounds rather than cancels itself out. The Tier 1 Civilian Protocol exists to solve this exact problem: how to build a body that remains capable across decades, not seasons.

The defining feature of durability is not strength alone. It is optional capacity. The ability to respond to life without negotiation. To lift when lifting is required. To carry when carrying is unavoidable. To move for hours when the day demands it. To recover overnight instead of over weeks. To remain capable when conditions are imperfect.

Most people do not realize how much of their future freedom is decided by what they can physically tolerate. Travel becomes shorter. Adventures become conditional. Plans shrink to match energy. Terrain dictates decisions. Life reorganizes itself around what the body will allow. This is not aging. It is unmanaged decline.

The Tier 1 Civilian Protocol is built to prevent that outcome.

It rejects the false choice between elite performance and casual fitness. It recognizes that most people do not need to be exceptional at one thing. They need to be competent at many things for a very long time. It prioritizes structural strength over cosmetic strength. Cardiovascular capacity over exhaustion. Mobility over stiffness. Core integrity over appearance.

This is not about doing more. It is about doing the right things consistently.

A durable body is not one that never breaks down. It is one

that adapts. It tolerates stress. It recovers quickly. It remains trainable. It does not require constant reinvention. The Tier 1 Civilian Protocol is designed to be repeatable across years, portable across environments, and resilient across life phases.

It also respects a critical truth: discipline must be sustainable to matter. A protocol that demands constant motivation will eventually fail. A protocol that integrates naturally into daily life compounds. Morning rucks. Simple strength sessions. Endurance that doubles as exploration. Mobility that protects rather than interrupts. This is fitness that integrates instead of competing with life.

Most importantly, the Tier 1 Civilian Protocol reframes fitness as stewardship. You are not training for an event. You are maintaining an asset. You are investing in a body that will carry your intellect, your work, your relationships, and your curiosity through the decades ahead. This shifts behavior from urgency to consistency, from intensity to intelligence.

The long game does not reward extremes. It rewards durability.

A body built this way does not announce itself. It simply works. It supports long days, long walks, long trips, and long thinking. It allows you to remain physically present in your own life. That presence becomes a quiet advantage.

This is the problem the Tier 1 Civilian Protocol is designed to solve. And it is why the structure matters more than the workout.

My own understanding of durability began long before I named it. In college, as an NCAA athlete, durability came naturally. I was strong because the environment required it. I was conditioned because the schedule demanded it. Youth concealed the fragility beneath the surface. But in my forties and early fifties, the illusion disappeared. Strength fades if you do not protect it. Mobility shrinks if you do not maintain it. Endurance declines if you do not cultivate it. What was once effortless now required intention. A knee surgery in my forties removed any remaining illusion of invincibility.

The Tier 1 Civilian Protocol was shaped through that realization. It emerged from rebuilding the foundation of my physical life, piece by piece, in a way that could last.

The protocol has four pillars.

The first is **strength**. Not bodybuilding. Not chasing numbers. Strength as capability. Being able to lift your body. Carry weight. Protect your joints. Maintain muscle mass that supports longevity. Strength is your insurance policy. It allows you to stay upright, stable, and resilient as the decades accumulate. It keeps you functional. It keeps you confident.

The second is **endurance**. Not in the competitive sense, but in the physiological sense. The ability to sustain effort. The ability to move for hours. The ability to recover quickly. For me, endurance has two expressions. Hiking with load and cycling. Hiking with load builds durability through sustained, weighted movement. It strengthens the hips, back, and core. It improves posture and stability. It teaches the body to work, slowly and steadily, across real terrain. Cycling builds the engine. It improves Zone 2 capacity, threshold strength, and cardiovascular efficiency. Hills push you toward your limits. Long, steady rides build the aerobic base that protects your future heart. Together, hiking with load and cycling create a form of endurance that is accessible, sustainable, and deeply effective.

The third is **mobility**. Mobility is the quiet pillar. The one most people skip. But mobility determines how long you can train without interruption. It determines how you recover. It determines how you move through the world. Mobility keeps the joints open, the tissues fluid, and the body capable of change. It protects the work you do in the other pillars. It allows strength and endurance to compound.

The fourth is **core integrity**. Not in the aesthetic sense, but in the structural sense. A strong core stabilizes everything else. It connects the upper and lower body. It supports hiking, cycling, lifting, and daily life. It prevents compensations that lead to injury. It keeps the system aligned.

Together, these four pillars create the Tier 1 Civilian Protocol. Strength. Endurance. Mobility. Core. Not complicated. Not extreme. But profoundly effective.

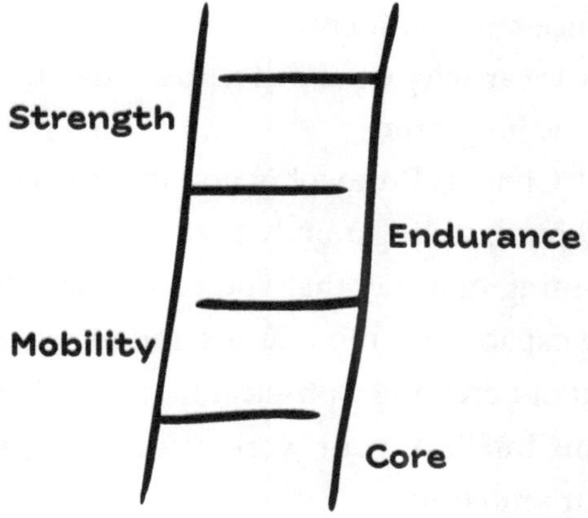

FIGURE 10 The Tier 1 Civilian Protocol
Strength, endurance, mobility, and core integrity work together to create a body that remains capable through every decade.

For someone in their twenties, the protocol builds a foundation that will serve every decade that follows. It teaches you that fitness is not a project. It is an identity. It allows you to accumulate capacity early and protect it as life becomes more complex. It slows the decline that so many assume is inevitable.

For someone in their fifties, the protocol becomes a pathway back. It allows you to rebuild strength with precision. It restores endurance without overloading the joints. It improves mobility in ways that reduce pain. It expands capacity at an age when most people believe they can only hold on to what they have. The body responds to intention at any age. The protocol proves it.

Durability is the real goal. Not peak performance. Not aesthetics. Not quick transformations. Durability is what allows you to hike with your children or grandchildren. Travel without fatigue. Cycle through the hills of Bucks County or the coastline of New England. Ruck through your neighborhood each morning. Carry your own luggage. Climb stairs. Move through life with competence and confidence.

Durability is capacity extended across time. It is the physical expression of the long game.

The Tier 1 Civilian Protocol is not about becoming an elite athlete. It is about building a body that enhances your freedom. It is about training in a way that you can sustain for decades. It is about being capable when it matters and recovering when you need to. It is about creating a physical foundation strong enough to support your intellect, your work, your travel, your relationships, and your ambitions.

In the end, this protocol is not about fitness. It is about stewardship. It is about honoring the quiet responsibility you owe to your future self. It is about building a chassis that will not fail under the weight of the life you want to live.

This is the Tier 1 Civilian Protocol.

The blueprint for a body that compounds.

CHAPTER 18
Daily Practice Reinforces Capability

Capability is the currency of a long life.

If there is one force that shapes a long, capable life more than any other, it is daily practice. Not goals. Not bursts of motivation. Not occasional intensity. Daily practice. The quiet rhythm you return to until it becomes identity. It is the engine that reinforces capability and an operating system that makes the rest of your life work.

Most people misunderstand this. They think transformation comes from breakthroughs or a single act of discipline. But durable change does not come from dramatic effort. It comes from small efforts repeated consistently. It comes from the structure you return to when life is uncertain. It comes from the habits that build your body, sharpen your mind, and protect your long-term vitality.

My own understanding of this took time. In my twenties, daily practice was built into my life as a student-athlete. Training was scheduled. Movement was mandatory. Capability was a byproduct of the environment. But decades later, when that structure disappeared, I realized how much I needed a deliberate rhythm to stay grounded, healthy, and clear.

That realization became sharper one quiet morning at home. I woke early, made coffee, and stepped outside for a short ruck. The air was cool and still. As I walked, my mind began to settle, and I could feel the day aligning before it had even begun. When I returned, I checked the sleep data from my Garmin dashboard. High sleep score. Strong recovery. A clear signal to train. It was simple, almost unremarkable. Yet it shaped the entire day. That morning reminded me why daily practice is not optional. It is foundational.

Daily practice is not about optimization. It is about reliability. The most important benefit of a daily rhythm is not what it adds, but what it removes. It removes negotiation. It removes friction. It removes the need to decide who you are each morning.

When practice becomes consistent, capability stops being something you hope to maintain and becomes something you expect. You no longer ask whether you should move today or read today or write today. You simply do. The behavior precedes motivation. Identity follows action.

The quiet danger of abandoning daily practice is not immediate decline. It is the slow return of randomness. Days begin to feel reactive. Movement becomes occasional. Reading becomes fragmented. Sleep drifts later and shorter. None of this feels dramatic. But capability erodes in the gaps between intention and action.

Daily practice closes those gaps.

With repetition, it becomes a form of insurance. When life becomes unpredictable, practice remains stable. When travel disrupts routines, you default to the essentials. When stress rises, the rhythm holds. You may shorten sessions. You may adjust intensity. But you do not abandon the structure. The practice flexes without breaking.

This is where most people misunderstand discipline. They believe consistency requires rigidity. In reality, durability comes from adaptability. A daily practice that only works in perfect conditions will fail precisely when it is needed most. A resilient practice is one that can survive fatigue, distraction, and constraint.

The measure of a good daily practice is not how impressive it looks on a calendar. It is how easily it reasserts itself after disruption.

This is why daily practice is best understood as a minimum viable rhythm. It is not everything you could do. It is the smallest set of actions that preserves capability. Enough movement to keep the body primed. Enough reading to keep the mind elastic. Enough writing to maintain clarity. Enough sleep to allow recovery. Enough restraint to avoid excess.

When the minimum is protected, intensity becomes optional rather than required.

Across long horizons, this rhythm produces a compounding effect that is difficult to appreciate in the short term. Capability built through daily practice does not stack linearly. It stacks structurally. Strength supports endurance. Endurance improves sleep. Sleep sharpens judgment. Better judgment protects habits. With consistency, the system begins to reinforce itself.

That reinforcement creates something more powerful than consistency alone. It creates momentum. Daily practice does not operate in silos; it operates as a system. When practice is continuous, progress compounds. When it is repeatedly interrupted, progress resets. The difference is not intensity, but continuity.

The diagram that follows makes this distinction visible. One path shows compounding momentum built through consistency. The other shows the familiar reset cycle of start, stop, recover, repeat. Both involve effort. Only one builds lasting capacity.

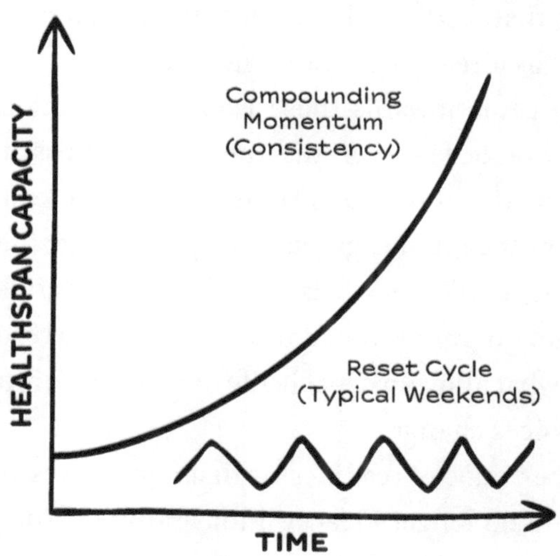

FIGURE 11 Compounding Momentum vs. the Reset Cycle

The pattern is rarely dramatic. For many people, this reset cycle is most visible on weekends. A disciplined week is followed by poorer food choices, disrupted sleep, and sometimes alcohol. None of this feels extreme in isolation. But the effect is cumulative. Progress made Monday through Friday is partially undone, not through excess, but through interruption. The issue is not indulgence. It is the loss of continuity.

When continuity is preserved, something subtle changes. Daily practice stops feeling like a decision that must be renegotiated and starts behaving like a default.

This is why daily practice eventually feels effortless. Not because it requires no effort, but because it requires no argument.

Daily practice also creates honesty. It provides constant feedback. If sleep degrades, you see it. If recovery slows, you feel it. If attention wanders, reading becomes harder. These signals arrive early, long before decline becomes visible. Practice gives you time to adjust while the margin still exists.

Without that feedback loop, most people do not notice erosion until it has already narrowed their options.

The long game rewards those who protect optionality. Daily practice is one of the few levers that preserves it across physical, cognitive, and emotional domains simultaneously. It keeps the body usable. It keeps the mind engaged. It keeps the inner life ordered.

This is why daily practice is not a habit. It is infrastructure.

It does not guarantee outcomes. It guarantees readiness. And readiness is what allows a capable life to continue unfolding, even as circumstances change.

The deeper value of readiness is that it preserves agency when conditions are no longer ideal. Viktor Frankl captured this with uncommon clarity when he wrote, *"When we are no longer able to change a situation, we are challenged to change ourselves."*[7]

Daily practice is how that challenge is met. It is the discipline that remains when motivation fades, when schedules tighten, and when circumstances stop cooperating. You may not control the season you are in, but you can control the posture you bring to it.

That posture needs feedback. One of the most revealing is sleep. It is one of the clearest indicators of both readiness and performance.

In *Why We Sleep*[8], neuroscientist Matthew Walker explains that sleep isn't just a passive state; it's active restoration. It clears metabolic waste from the brain, consolidates memory, strengthens the immune system, and regulates the hormones that control appetite, energy, and stress. When my sleep score is high, everything else improves. My training is sharper. My mind is steadier. My decisions are more precise. I've come to see sleep not just as recovery, but as strategy.

My daily practice has several parts, each reinforcing capability in a different way.

It begins with movement. Some mornings it is a ruck. Other mornings it's a bike ride along familiar routes that allow for steady cadence and quiet thought. Cycling has become one of the most powerful parts of my vitality practice. The rhythm of breath. The Zone 2 engine work. The natural threshold training that emerges on hills. It strengthens the heart, sharpens attention, and builds the aerobic foundation that protects longevity.

Movement steadies the body. Reading steadies the mind. Not scanning or skimming but real reading. It keeps my mind sharp. How I introduce new ideas. How I create mental range. Reading is also a form of prevention. Reading reshapes the brain in ways that persist across a lifetime, strengthening neural pathways and protecting long-term cognitive health.[9] For me, reading is vitality work.

Writing completes the loop. It is not something I do for productivity. It is my method of thinking. It is how I refine the questions I am wrestling with. It is how I organize ideas and identify patterns. Writing keeps the mind agile. It forces coherence. It strengthens cognition in the same way movement strengthens the body.

Nutrition follows the same principle of simplicity. I aim for roughly 2,500 calories a day. Enough to maintain strength, support movement, and sustain energy without drifting into excess. Maintaining a healthy body composition is not about appearance. It is about protecting the joints. Lower body fat reduces inflammation, improves mobility, and makes physical activity easier. It is one of the quiet foundations of long-term capability.

And finally, sleep holds everything together. I track it daily through my Garmin device and dashboard. Not as a score to chase, but as a reflection of recovery. Deep sleep. REM sleep. Resting heart rate. HRV. These metrics show whether the system is primed for intensity or needs restoration. Sleep is not a luxury. It is the repair mechanism that makes the rest of the practice sustainable.

For someone in their twenties, daily practice is identity formation. It creates discipline early. It sets the trajectory for the decades ahead. It builds structure before life becomes crowded. It allows the mind and body to grow in alignment.

For someone in their fifties and beyond, daily practice becomes a stabilizer. It reintroduces order. It creates reliability. It rebuilds capability that may have eroded across the years. It restores the confidence that improvement is still available. It anchors you to a rhythm that can carry you forward with intention.

Daily practice also removes decision fatigue. When something becomes part of your identity, it no longer requires negotiation. You wake. You move. You read. You write. You eat well.

You sleep. These are not chores. They are acts of self-respect. They are commitments to your future self.

The real power of daily practice is that it reinforces capability from all angles. Physical, cognitive, and emotional capability. It expands the life you are able to live. It protects your autonomy. It strengthens the slope of your future.

Daily practice is not about perfection. It is about direction. It is the quiet force that shapes your body, sharpens your mind, and extends your freedom.

CHAPTER 19
The Longevity Playbook

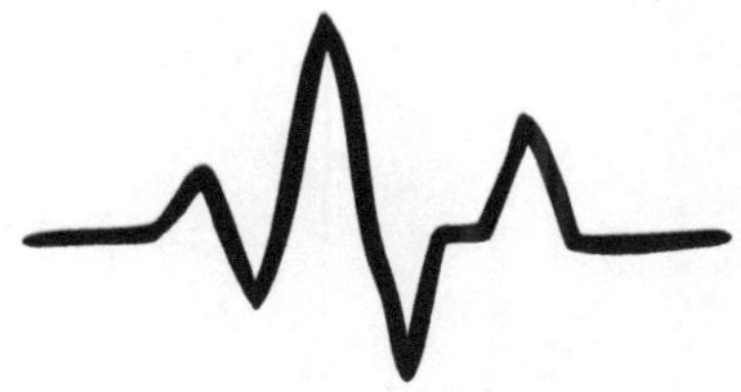

Longevity is not accidental. It is designed.

L ongevity is not built through isolated habits. It emerges from systems. From the way individual practices are designed to reinforce one another. What matters is not whether you lift, sleep, eat well, or think deeply in isolation, but whether these elements are arranged in a structure that compounds rather than competes.

For years, I approached health the way many people do, as a collection of separate efforts. Strength lived in one lane. Endurance in another. Nutrition, sleep, and thinking somewhere off to the side. Each mattered, but none fully delivered on its own. The breakthrough came not from adding more discipline, but from designing a system where each part strengthened the others.

That system is what I call the Longevity Playbook.

Where daily practice provides rhythm, the Playbook provides architecture. It explains *why* certain practices matter, *how* they connect, and *what* makes them durable across decades rather than seasons.

The reason most longevity efforts fail is not lack of effort. It is fragmentation. People do many of the right things, but they do them in isolation. Strength without endurance. Endurance without recovery. Nutrition without training context. Thinking without physical vitality. Each element, taken alone, appears sensible. Together, they fail to compound.

Fragmentation creates hidden friction. Strength sessions leave the body inflamed because sleep is insufficient. Endurance erodes muscle because nutrition is misaligned. Cognitive work becomes sluggish because recovery is shallow. None of this feels dramatic in the moment. But the system leaks energy. Progress stalls. Motivation fades. The individual parts remain, but the structure weakens.

This is why longevity cannot be approached as a checklist. It must be designed as an ecosystem, where each element lowers the cost of the others rather than competing for attention.

When strength, endurance, mobility, sleep, nutrition, and cognitive engagement are aligned, something subtle but powerful occurs. The burden of effort decreases. Training becomes easier to recover from. Thinking becomes clearer with less strain. Discipline requires less force because the system itself is doing more of the work. The architecture begins to support itself.

This is the defining advantage of a playbook over a routine.

A routine asks for compliance. A playbook creates leverage by design.

Sleep illustrates this distinction clearly. Treated in isolation, it is often reduced to a score to optimize or a habit to fix. Within the Playbook, sleep becomes regulatory. It determines training intensity, informs recovery decisions, and shapes cognitive output. It is no longer passive. It becomes directional.

Strength changes character as well. Within the system, it stops being about sessions or numbers and becomes protective. It preserves mobility, supports endurance, stabilizes joints, and maintains independence. Strength shifts from performance to resilience, and that shift matters more with each passing decade.

Endurance, too, is reframed. It stops being about suffering or speed and becomes about capacity. A strong aerobic base lowers the perceived cost of effort across daily life. Recovery accelerates. Stress tolerance improves. Endurance widens the margin within which everything else operates.

Mobility acts as connective tissue. It determines whether gains accumulate or decay. Without it, progress is borrowed. With it, progress compounds.

Nutrition, when properly placed, becomes structural rather

than emotional. It fuels training, supports recovery, and maintains body composition without becoming a source of identity or control. Food serves the system instead of dominating it.

Cognitive engagement completes the loop. A body trained without a mind that remains engaged eventually stagnates. Reading and writing preserve curiosity, sharpen attention, and protect long-term cognition. They reinforce the mental resilience required to sustain physical discipline over decades. In the Playbook, thinking is treated as training, not an accessory.

When these elements are aligned, life begins to feel lighter. Decisions require less negotiation. Energy returns more quickly. Capability becomes dependable rather than fragile. What many people experience as motivation is, in truth, coherence.

Fragmented systems rely on willpower. Integrated systems rely on design.

Over decades, this distinction matters more than any single habit. The Longevity Playbook does not promise peak performance. It promises continuity. It preserves the ability to travel, train, think, explore, and create across changing seasons of life. It allows ambition to evolve without physical betrayal.

This is why longevity must be treated as infrastructure. When health is designed as a system, it stops competing with the rest of life and begins supporting it. Capability expands instead of contracts. And the long game becomes something you can actually sustain.

At its core, the Playbook is built around a small number of non-negotiable elements, each chosen for its ability to reinforce the others.

Strength forms the foundation. It preserves muscle, protects joints, and keeps the body structurally resilient as the years accumulate. Strength is not about performance or aesthetics. It is about maintaining a body that can support movement, absorb stress, and remain stable across time. Without strength, the rest of the system degrades.

Endurance sits alongside it as the engine. Cardiorespiratory fitness, particularly VO_2 max, is one of the strongest predictors of long-term health and independence. Endurance expands the bandwidth of daily life. It allows effort without fatigue, recovery without fragility, and movement without limitation. A strong engine widens the margin for everything else.

Mobility connects these pillars. It is the difference between strength that lasts and strength that breaks down. Mobility keeps joints open, tissues adaptable, and movement fluid. It allows strength and endurance to compound rather than collide. Small, consistent investments here prevent large interruptions later.

Nutrition is not treated as optimization, but as alignment. Its role is to support training, recovery, and body composition without becoming a source of friction or excess. Food, in this system, is structural, not emotional, moral, or performative. It keeps the system calibrated.

Sleep anchors everything. It is the stabilizing force beneath the entire architecture. Recovery determines whether effort compounds or collapses. Deep sleep, REM sleep, heart rate, and HRV do not serve as targets to chase, but as signals that reveal whether the system is working. Sleep does not accelerate progress. It preserves it.

Cognitive engagement completes the loop. Reading and writing are not intellectual hobbies layered on top of physical life. They are protective forces. They sharpen attention, strengthen memory, and preserve cognitive range. In a long game measured in decades, mental vitality is inseparable from physical vitality.

Intellectual engagement is also one of the strongest protective factors against neurodegenerative decline. Having seen the cost of diseases like Alzheimer's and Parkinson's up close, I treat reading and writing as part of my vitality strategy, not as optional pursuits. They are elements of healthspan, helping preserve cognitive function, sustain curiosity, and keep the mind adaptive as the years accumulate.

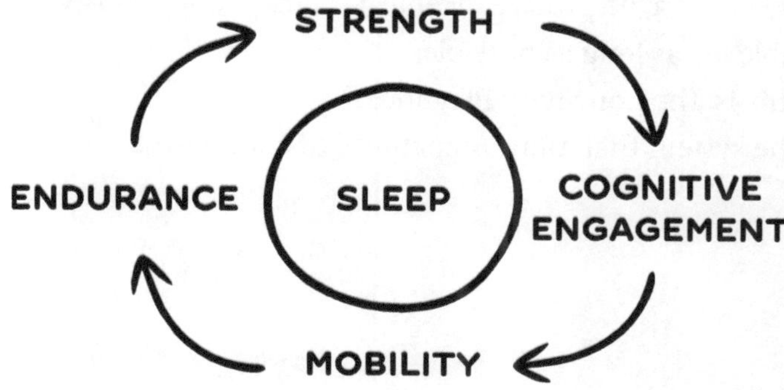

FIGURE 12 The Longevity Playbook
The diagram shows how the core elements of longevity reinforce one another. Sleep anchors the system; strength, endurance, mobility, and cognitive engagement form the cycle that compounds.

What distinguishes The Longevity Playbook from a routine is not intensity, but coherence. When these elements are aligned, the system becomes self-reinforcing. Strength improves endurance. Endurance improves recovery. Recovery sharpens thinking. Clear thinking improves decisions around training, nutrition, and life. The parts stop competing for attention and begin amplifying one another.

For someone early in life, the Playbook establishes a structure that prevents erosion before it begins. For someone later in life, it becomes a method of renewal, not by reclaiming youth, but by restoring capability.

Longevity is not accidental. It is designed. Not through rigidity, but through alignment. Not through optimization, but through stewardship.

The Longevity Playbook is not a program to follow. It is a framework to inhabit. A way of organizing effort so that the body and mind improve together, predictably.

The goal is simple:

To build a life where strength, clarity, and energy remain available for as long as possible.

This is The Longevity Playbook.

The system that allows capability to compound.

CHAPTER 20

Built to Compound

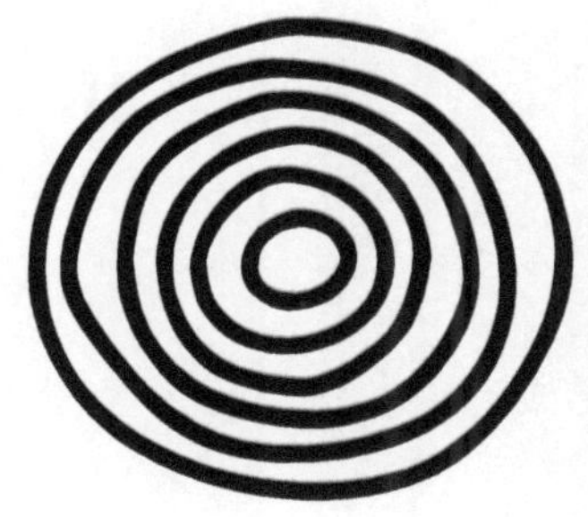

Health is not a phase of life. It is the infrastructure beneath it.

There is a moment in every person's life when they realize that the body they carry determines the life they are able to live. Not in an aesthetic sense. Not in pursuit of performance metrics. But in the simplest possible terms. Your body is the instrument through which you experience the world. It is the vehicle for your work, your relationships, your ambitions, and your freedom. It shapes the energy you bring to each day and the way you feel as the years accumulate. When you understand this, you begin to see your body the same way you see your finances or your mind. Something that compounds.

Building a body that improves is not about intensity. It isn't about chasing peaks. It is about creating a trajectory. The body responds to consistency. It adapts to attention. It reshapes itself in response to what you do repeatedly. The further I move into this long-game philosophy, the more I realize that my physical life is not defined by any single year. It is defined by the slope across decades.

I experienced this shift gradually. There was no dramatic turning point. Just a pattern. When I recommitted to strength, mobility, endurance, nutrition, and sleep, my body responded. When I treated training as an identity rather than a task, the trend line changed. Over months and years, capability returned. Strength rebuilt. VO_2 max climbed. Recovery improved. The increases were not explosive. They were steady. Predictable. Compounding.

Compounding in the body follows the same laws as compounding anywhere else. Early inputs matter more than late ones. Consistency matters more than intensity. Interruptions matter more than missed days. And systems outperform willpower every time.

What most people misunderstand about physical decline is its cause. They assume the body breaks down because of age, when in reality it breaks down because of neglect, volatility, and long stretches without signal. Muscle is not lost suddenly. Aerobic capacity does not disappear overnight. Mobility does not vanish in a single season. These capacities erode when they are no longer asked for. The body adapts downward just as faithfully as it adapts upward.

A body that compounds is one that remains in steady conversation with effort. Not maximal effort, but repeated, intelligent stress followed by adequate recovery. This is the biological equivalent of long-term investing. Each training session deposits a small amount of stimulus. Each night of quality sleep compounds it. Each week of repetition builds structural resilience. The return curve bends upward.

The inverse is equally true. Long layoffs, erratic training, and reactive bursts create volatility. They feel productive in the moment but produce fragility. Injury risk rises. Recovery slows. Confidence erodes. Eventually, the system begins to feel unreliable, and the person pulls back—not because they intend to, but because the body no longer feels trustworthy. This is how decline accelerates without a clear inflection point.

What distinguishes physical compounding from financial compounding is the immediacy of feedback. The body continuously reports what is working. Resting heart rate trends. Recovery quality. Joint comfort. Energy throughout the day. Training either feels sustainable or brittle. The signal is always present, but it only becomes useful when someone is paying attention long enough to recognize the pattern.

This is where identity plays a decisive role. When training is something you do, it competes with everything else. When it is part of who you are, it becomes structural. The body responds most reliably to what is repeated without friction. Identity removes friction. It turns effort into routine, routine into structure, and structure into durability.

Another overlooked requirement for compounding is margin. A body trained perpetually at the edge of exhaustion cannot compound; it can only survive. Progress requires surplus. Enough sleep to recover. Enough nutrition to adapt. Enough restraint to avoid chronic inflammation and overuse. This is not about doing less. It is about doing the right amount, consistently, for a very long time.

As the years pass, the benefits become nonlinear. Strength protects joints and connective tissue. Aerobic capacity improves metabolic health, blood pressure, and cognitive clarity. High-quality sleep accelerates recovery across every system. These gains reinforce one another, creating a flywheel effect. Movement becomes easier. Effort feels lighter. Capability expands instead of contracts.

Most importantly, a body that compounds preserves optionality. It allows you to say yes to trips that involve long walks, uneven terrain, lifting, or sustained effort. It allows you to work full days without exhaustion, to travel without accumulating recovery debt, and to age without steadily shrinking your world.

This is the real return on investment. Not aesthetics. Not performance milestones. But freedom of movement, confidence in capacity, and trust in the system you have built.

Over decades, this approach creates a quiet advantage. While others are managing limitations, you are managing opportunity. While others are protecting energy, you are deploying it. While others are negotiating with their bodies, yours is cooperating.

A body that compounds does not resist time. It works with

it. It accepts that the slope matters more than the peak, and that durability outperforms intensity across every meaningful horizon.

This is how vitality becomes an asset rather than a concern. Not through ambition, but through stewardship. Not through urgency, but through alignment. Not by chasing youth, but by building capacity that lasts.

This is what most people miss. The body is extraordinarily responsive, even later in life. The idea that you must accept decline at forty or fifty or sixty is a myth. The research is clear. Strength can be rebuilt. Muscle can be added. Endurance can be improved. VO_2 max can climb. Mobility can return. Recovery can strengthen. The body is not static; it is adaptive. It reflects what you ask of it consistently.

For someone in their twenties, this chapter is an invitation. Build capacity early. Strengthen the foundation now. You will never regret the hours you invested in your body. You will only regret the years you assumed youth would last forever. Compounding does not begin at midlife. It begins the moment you decide who you want to be.

For someone in their fifties and beyond, this chapter is permission. You are not too late. Your body is not done adapting. Your best years of capability can still be ahead of you. When you combine intelligence, structure, and consistency, the improvements feel almost disproportionate. Strength returns quickly. Endurance rises reliably. Sleep deepens. Energy stabilizes. The body responds to effort long after people assume it cannot.

The path to building a body that compounds is simple, but simple does not mean trivial. It means essential. Strength training a few days a week. Mobility work that keeps the joints open. Nutrition that sustains energy without drifting into excess. Sleep that repairs the system. And for me, a consistent target of roughly two hundred minutes of cardiovascular work each week. Some of that time is spent in steady Zone 2, building the aerobic base that protects longevity. Some of it is spent at higher intensities, pushing my threshold and challenging the system to adapt. Cycling, rucking, hills, and occasional high-output sessions create a balance that keeps the engine strong and responsive.

All of these components reinforce one another. Strength improves endurance. Endurance improves sleep. Sleep improves recovery. Recovery improves training quality. Nutrition accelerates adaptation. Mobility keeps everything functioning smoothly. Reading and writing sharpen focus, which improves the discipline required to maintain the routine. When you combine these elements, a system emerges. A life designed around capability.

The goal is not to become exceptional. The goal is to become durable. A durable body is one that can handle travel, stress, long days, heavy loads, unexpected challenges, and the simple demands of living. Durability keeps you independent. It keeps you engaged. It keeps you exploring. It keeps you in motion. Durability is freedom.

What I have learned is that compounding is not only a financial principle. It applies just as powerfully to the body. The small choices you make today determine the strength, energy, and vitality you will have decades from now. The habits you repeat become your physical identity. The way you treat your body now determines the life you will be able to live later.

A body that compounds is not built in a season. It is built across a lifetime. It is built through a rhythm you return to. It is built through a respect for the future. It is built through daily practice, intelligent training, aligned nutrition, restorative sleep, and a mindset oriented around the long game.

This is where vitality comes into focus. Vitality is not separate from intellect or capital. It is the multiplier. It is the force that amplifies every other part of your life. When your body is strong, your mind sharpens. When your mind sharpens, your financial decisions improve. When your financial decisions improve, your life gains freedom. Health is not a domain. It is the chassis that supports all other domains.

A body that compounds is a life that compounds.

This is the path.

This is the long game.

CHAPTER 21
The Road Ahead

A well-designed life expands with age instead of narrowing beneath its demands.

With time, a life begins to reveal its underlying design. What once felt scattered starts to arrange itself into a pattern you can finally see. The long game shifts from a framework you try to follow into a rhythm you gradually inhabit, and the path ahead takes shape not through certainty but through clarity. The decisions, disciplines, and experiences accumulated across decades begin to align, and the future becomes less about prediction and more about direction.

For much of adulthood, progress is mistaken for speed. We chase accomplishments, compress timelines, and assume urgency will deliver meaning. Yet the most durable forms of growth rarely come from acceleration. They emerge from the slow accrual of choices that compound in the background: the strengthening of the body, the sharpening of the mind, the stewardship of capital, the steady shaping of character. These forces begin to support one another, and what once required conscious effort becomes structural. Capacity deepens. Perspective matures. Strength gains roots.

This is where the long game reveals its true power. Intellect, capital, and vitality, the three pillars that shape the architecture of a meaningful life, begin to converge instead of competing for space. In youth, they exist in fragments: intellect is still forming, capital is scarce, and vitality is abundant but unfocused. With experience, they start to reinforce each other. Your knowledge refines your decisions. Your capital provides the freedom to pursue what matters. Your vitality allows you to sustain the habits that carry you forward. Together, they create a life that expands with age rather than contracts beneath its demands.

Compounding sits at the center of this expansion. Not just financial compounding, though that remains an extraordinary force, but the compounding of attention, resilience, relationships, and insight. We compound our understanding by reading deeply and thinking clearly. We compound our health through practices that preserve mobility, strength, and clarity across decades. We compound our opportunities by placing ourselves in environments and conversations that elevate our trajectory. As these forms of compounding interact, they generate alignment, the quiet state in which your life begins to reflect what you value most.

Viewed through this lens, the question of the road ahead changes. It becomes less about what you hope to accomplish and more about who you are becoming, and whether the structure of your life supports that evolution. Achievement fades quickly; alignment does not. When intellect, capital, and vitality are integrated, the future opens rather than closes. You are no longer driven by the pursuit of more, but by the pursuit of what matters. That shift changes how the road ahead must be built.

Preparing yourself for the life ahead is not an abstract exercise. It is a daily, cumulative act. It happens through the systems you build, the disciplines you return to, and the standards you maintain when no one is watching. The long game reveals itself not in dramatic reinvention, but in the steady refinement of how you live.

What distinguishes this stage of life is that the inputs finally begin to matter more than the outcomes. Earlier decades reward visible progress. Titles, income, milestones, and markers of advancement offer clear feedback. But those signals lose their usefulness. They tell you where you have been, not whether the structure of your life is capable of carrying you forward. At this point, success becomes less about accumulation and more about coherence.

Coherence is the alignment between how you spend your days and the future you are shaping. It is the integration of intellect, capital, and vitality into a system that supports rather than strains you. When these elements operate in isolation, life feels busy and fragmented. When they reinforce one another, effort becomes quieter, and progress becomes more durable.

This is where many people subtly drift. They continue optimizing individual parts of their lives without stepping back to examine the whole. They invest intelligently but neglect their health. They build physical strength but allow their intellectual life to narrow. They gain freedom on paper but structure their days in ways that feel constraining. None of these choices are catastrophic. But misalignment compounds just as surely as discipline does.

The long game demands a different posture. It asks you to design for endurance rather than intensity. To prioritize systems over spurts of effort. To build a life that grows easier to sustain as the years advance, rather than harder. This is not a retreat from ambition. It is a refinement of it.

At this stage, clarity becomes the most valuable asset you can cultivate. Clarity about what you are no longer optimizing for. Clarity about which inputs truly matter. Clarity about the tradeoffs you are willing to make, and the ones you are not. This kind of clarity does not arrive through force. It emerges through reflection, through attention, and through a willingness to simplify.

Simplification is often misunderstood as reduction. In reality, it is concentration. It is the act of removing friction so that energy can flow where it matters most. Financial simplicity reduces cognitive load. Physical consistency preserves capacity. Intellectual engagement maintains range. Together, they create margin, and margin creates freedom.

This is also the point where compounding becomes deeply personal. Not the abstract mathematics of growth, but the lived experience of momentum. When your health supports your curiosity. When your capital supports your choices. When your routines reinforce rather than drain you. The days begin to stack in your favor. You are no longer fighting entropy at every turn. You are cooperating with it.

The road ahead, seen this way, is not a narrowing path. It is a widening one. Not because options multiply endlessly, but because you have built the capacity to choose well among them. You become less reactive, less rushed, and less compelled to prove anything. In its place emerges a quieter confidence: the sense that your life is structurally sound.

This is the true promise of the long game. Not certainty, but preparedness. Not perfection, but durability. A life designed to evolve without breaking, to deepen without hardening, and to remain responsive to what matters most.

From here, the question is no longer how much more you can add. It is whether what you have built is aligned enough to carry you forward with clarity, strength, and purpose. When that alignment is in place, movement stops being reactive and becomes exploratory.

At this stage of life, exploration becomes essential. Tolkien's line, *"Not all those who wander are lost"*, captures a truth that grows more relevant with time.[10] Exploration is not a lack of direction; it is a method of renewal. It keeps the mind elastic, the body engaged, and the spirit awake. It disrupts stagnation. It reconnects you to curiosity. It reminds you that the world remains larger than your routines, and that you remain capable of expanding alongside it.

This is one reason I return to the mountains in Vermont. There is a rhythm I have come to know well—early mornings before the lifts grow crowded, when the mountain is still holding the night. I clip into my skis and push off for a first run, the air sharp enough to wake every part of me. Halfway down, the trees open and the valley comes into view, the light just beginning to rise over the ridgeline, soft and unhurried.

Nothing dramatic happens in these moments, yet something essential always reveals itself. As I carve through the quiet, the years behind me do not feel fixed; they feel foundational. And the years ahead, however many remain, feel wide, almost untouched. It becomes clear that a life, like a mountain, does not reveal its shape through speed but through presence. Clarity arrives not in the rush of achievement, but in the stillness where you become aware of who you are becoming. It is a simple ritual, but one that continues to recalibrate me, a reminder that exploration is not about distance, but about attention.

In this way, exploration becomes the purest expression of the intellectual pillar of the long game, a commitment to remain teachable, curious, open to refinement. Capital takes on a new meaning as well. Financial resources matter less for what they allow you to purchase and more for the freedom they grant you. Capital becomes a tool for alignment, a means of shaping the life you want to inhabit rather than impressing anyone else. Reputation, judgment, time autonomy, and optionality become forms of wealth that compound just as powerfully as returns in a portfolio.

Vitality remains the foundation that determines the range of possibilities available to you. Strength, mobility, sleep, energy, and clarity form the chassis that supports everything else. A long life without vitality is constraint; a long life with vitality is possibility. It is the platform on which the next decade, and the decades after that, stand.

When these three forces work together, the road ahead becomes less about managing decline and more about optimizing potential. You begin to craft a life that is durable, spacious, and purposeful, one that can hold ambition without anxiety, discipline without rigidity, and growth without chaos. The long game transforms from a strategy for achievement into a method for living.

So what does the road ahead look like?

It looks like a horizon informed by coherence rather than haste.

It looks like a future shaped by compounding rather than intensity.

It looks like a continued commitment to becoming someone capable of carrying a meaningful life across decades.

The road ahead is long, and that is its greatest advantage. It gives you room to evolve, to deepen your perspective, to refine your purpose, and to wander with intention. It invites you to apply the principles that shaped the earlier chapters of your life with even greater precision in the chapters still to come.

May the years ahead widen your horizon, sharpen your intellect, strengthen your vitality, and expand your capital in all the ways that matter. And may they remind you consistently that the long game is not something you complete. It is something you continue, shaped by who you are becoming and the choices you compound from here.

CONCLUSION

There is a moment late in any long journey when you can finally see how the pieces fit together. It never arrives in your twenties. Rarely in your thirties. Sometimes in your forties. Almost always in your fifties. It is the moment when your life becomes coherent. When your decisions, disciplines, and experiences stop feeling separate and begin to feel connected. When the long game is no longer an idea. It is how you live.

For me, this realization arrived gradually, through accumulation rather than epiphany. Over years of notes, books, conversations, and lived experience, patterns began to surface. Ideas I had captured in passing on flights, in margins, during transitions started to connect. What once felt like isolated threads revealed a larger design. Curiosity had shaped how I thought. Discipline had strengthened how I lived. Stewardship had ordered my financial life. Together, they produced a form of quiet freedom I did not fully understand until it was already in place.

This is what the long game becomes when you stay with it. Not a plan. Not a list. A way of moving through the world.

As I look toward the years ahead, I do not think in terms of goals or deadlines. I think in terms of direction. I want to remain someone who grows intellectually, physically, and financially.

Someone who stays curious. Someone who stays strong. Someone who uses time as an ally rather than an adversary. Someone who continues to explore, learn, mentor, write, and contribute with clarity and energy. I want my life to keep becoming simpler, deeper, and more aligned.

The long game has something to offer at every age.

For someone in their twenties, the message is simple. Stay curious. Curiosity compounds. Learn widely. Build a body that can carry you for decades. Protect your attention. Avoid the trap of urgency. You do not need everything now. What you need is integrity, direction, and patience. Small decisions made early become enormous advantages later.

For someone in their fifties and beyond, the message is different but no less powerful. Stay capable. Reinvention is a form of strength. Your best physical years can still be ahead. Your most important intellectual contributions may still be forming. Your financial life can shift from accumulation to autonomy. This season of life is not a decline. It is a leverage point. Treat it that way.

What I have learned is that mind, money, and muscle all compound along the same curve. They grow slowly, then suddenly. They expand subtly, then obviously. They sharpen one another. A strong body gives you the energy to think clearly. A sharp mind strengthens your financial decisions. A resilient financial foundation gives you the freedom to build the physical and intellectual life you want. When all three compound together, life takes on a different quality. Decisions become easier. Stress becomes lower. Confidence grows. Time works for you.

In the years ahead, I want to share this philosophy with others who are on a similar path. A long game fellowship will be part of my future. A small group of people who believe in growth across decades. People who are disciplined, curious, and committed to designing their lives with intention. People who understand that excellence is quieter than it appears from the outside. People who want to surround themselves with others who value strength, clarity, exploration, and stewardship. Finding your tribe matters. It can change the trajectory of your life as much as any habit or skill.

This book is part of that vision. It is a record of the ideas, rhythms, and lessons that have shaped my life. It is my way of capturing what I have learned so far and offering it to anyone who wants to build a life that compounds. Something meant to endure beyond trends and remain useful to anyone, at any age, who wants to live deliberately.

If there is one truth I hope you carry with you, it is this. The long game is not about perfection. It is about orientation. You do not need to predict the future. You only need to move steadily toward it.

A good life is built the way anything strong is built—patiently, over years. With intention. With discipline. With curiosity. With care.

This is the long game: your mind, your capital, your body, your future all compounding together across a lifetime.

And it begins every morning.

AFTERWORD

As the years accumulate, a life begins to reveal what it was really shaped by. Not the moments that felt urgent, nor the decisions that drew attention at the time, but the forces that operated in the background. The habits you returned to. The standards you held when no one was watching. The posture you adopted toward time itself. Looking back, it becomes clear that most lives are not defined by dramatic pivots, but by the direction they held for long stretches.

This book was never meant to prescribe a perfect path. It was meant to illuminate a way of thinking. A way of orienting yourself toward a life that compounds rather than fragments. A life where intellect, capital, and vitality are not pursued in isolation, but designed to reinforce one another across decades. If there is a single thread running through every chapter, it is this: the most meaningful progress happens when your systems are aligned with who you are becoming, not who you are trying to impress.

Much of modern life encourages the opposite. Speed over direction. Optimization over coherence. Visibility over substance. We are trained to ask what more we can add rather than whether what we have built is stable enough to carry us forward.

The long game invites a different question. Not how fast can I move, but how well does my life hold together as time passes.

That distinction matters more than it appears.

In earlier chapters, the emphasis was on building foundations. Attention before ambition. Reading before opinion. Writing before certainty. Mental models before momentum. These practices are not ends in themselves. They are methods of sharpening judgment. Through accumulation, judgment becomes one of the rarest forms of leverage. It determines not just what you pursue, but what you ignore. And what you ignore often matters more.

The same principle applies to wealth. Money, left unattended, tends to pull identity toward it. It becomes a scoreboard. A proxy for worth. A source of noise. When designed intentionally, however, capital becomes quieter with time. It recedes into the background and supports the life you want to live rather than demanding to be managed constantly. The difference is not the amount. It is the structure.

The chapters on portfolio design, income stacking, tax planning, and the micro family office were not about cleverness. They were about reducing friction. They were about creating systems that free attention instead of consuming it. Over decades, attention becomes the scarcest asset you have. A well-designed financial life protects it.

Vitality follows the same arc. Health is often treated as a short-term project, something to address when it becomes inconvenient or visible. The long game treats vitality as infrastructure. The body is not separate from the rest of life. It is the chassis that carries every intention forward. Strength, endurance, mobility, sleep, and cognitive engagement are not pursuits of youth. They are commitments to continuity.

What becomes clear with time is that decline is rarely abrupt. It is gradual. It arrives through small accommodations that feel reasonable in the moment. You stop doing certain things because they feel slightly harder. You plan less because recovery takes longer. Possibility narrows. A longevity mindset resists this not through intensity, but through consistency. Through practices that keep capability available year after year.

Taken together, these elements form something larger than a set of habits. They form a way of living that is oriented toward durability. Toward lives that expand with age rather than contract beneath their own complexity. This is what the long game ultimately points toward. Not a finish line, but a posture.

One of the quieter lessons that emerges after decades is that alignment matters more than achievement. Achievement is fleeting. It spikes and fades. Alignment endures. When your daily practices, financial decisions, and intellectual life are pointed in the same direction, effort feels lighter. Progress becomes steadier. You stop needing constant reinforcement from the outside because your life begins to make sense from the inside.

This is also where exploration reenters the picture. Not as distraction, but as renewal. Exploration is not the absence of direction. It is what keeps direction from becoming rigid. It keeps the mind elastic, the body engaged, and curiosity alive. With experience, it becomes less about distance and more about attention. About staying open to refinement.

The road ahead, when viewed through this lens, becomes less about what you hope to accomplish and more about the life you are preparing yourself to live. A life supported by systems rather than sustained by willpower. A life where strength, clarity, and autonomy remain available even as circumstances change.

That future is not built all at once. It is assembled through small, repeatable decisions. Through reading that stretches you. Writing that clarifies you. Training that keeps you capable. Financial structures that reduce noise. Communities that reinforce standards rather than erode them. None of these choices are dramatic in isolation. Together, they shape a life that holds.

If there is an invitation embedded in these pages, it is not to copy a framework, but to design your own. To ask where your attention leaks. Where complexity has crept in unnoticed. Where alignment could replace effort. The long game looks different for every person, but the principles remain surprisingly stable. Favor depth over speed. Structure over impulse. Stewardship over display.

It is also worth saying this plainly: there will be seasons where progress feels invisible. Compounding works that way. The early stages are quiet. The benefits are delayed. The temptation to abandon what is working for something more stimulating is strong. This is true in investing. It is true in training. It is true in thinking. The long game rewards patience precisely because patience is so often in short supply.

Eventually, however, the effects become unmistakable. Decisions get cleaner. Recovery improves. Optionality widens. Life feels less reactive. You are no longer building from scratch each season. You are building on a foundation that has been reinforced repeatedly.

That foundation does not make life predictable. It makes it resilient.

Perhaps the most important realization that comes with time is that no one ever truly finishes the long game. There is no final chapter where everything is resolved. There is only continuation. Refinement. Recommitment. Each decade asks different questions. Each season shifts the emphasis. What remains constant is the need for clarity, capability, and care.

If this book has done its job, it has not given you answers to follow, but lenses to look through. A way to evaluate choices. A way to think beyond the immediate. A way to design a life that remains coherent as it evolves.

The road ahead is long. That is not a burden. It is an advantage. It gives you time to compound what matters. To correct course without panic. To deepen rather than rush. To live deliberately rather than urgently.

The long game is not something you complete. It is something you inhabit.

And with attention, alignment, and patience, it becomes a life that holds.

APPENDIX

Introduction to Frameworks

The frameworks that follow serve a different purpose than the chapters that precede them.

The main body of this book is narrative. It is reflective by design. It moves forward deliberately, building perspective through experience, example, and synthesis. It is meant to be read in sequence, absorbed gradually, and revisited selectively.

The frameworks operate differently. They are not meant to be read straight through or consumed in a single sitting. They are designed to be returned to. Consulted out of order. Held alongside real decisions and revisited as circumstances evolve. Where the narrative establishes orientation, the frameworks provide structure.

They are tools. The chapters introduce the architecture. The Appendix clarifies how the pieces connect. These frameworks are not meant to add complexity, but to reduce it. Each stands on its own. Together, they form a system you can return to as circumstances change.

On the Placement of Frameworks

Placing the frameworks after the core manuscript is intentional. Without narrative, a framework risks hardening into rules or slogans, divorced from the lived complexity it was meant to clarify. Context matters. So does perspective. The chapters that precede this Appendix supply that grounding.

At the same time, narrative without structure can remain abstract. Insight is felt, but not anchored. Patterns are sensed, but not named. Understanding fades when it lacks form.

The frameworks exist to resolve that tension.

They are not checklists. They are instruments of calibration. A framework does not make decisions for you. It refines the way you see them. Used consistently, it sharpens judgment by revealing patterns that would otherwise remain invisible.

They translate lived insight into durable architecture. They give shape to recurring patterns across health, wealth, learning, and long-term life design. Patterns that remain stable even as surface details change. They do not replace the narrative. They simply distill it.

What Earns a Framework a Place Here

None of the frameworks in this Appendix are included because they are novel.

Novelty is short-lived. It attracts attention, but rarely survives long horizons. A framework earns its place here only if it remains useful when incentives shift, when conditions change, and when short-term clarity gives way to uncertainty.

Durability is the filter.

Each framework reflects a pattern that has repeated itself across decades, cycles, and domains. Not once or briefly, but repeatedly across markets, bodies, careers, and lives.

Some of these patterns are obvious in hindsight. Others are easy to ignore in the moment. The purpose of a framework is not to make something clever, but to make something visible sooner.

How to Read This Section

You do not need to read this Appendix linearly. In fact, you are better off not doing so.

Each framework is self-contained. You can return to one without consulting the others. You can ignore several entirely for long stretches of time. That is not a failure of the frameworks. It is how they are meant to be used.

At the same time, the frameworks are not independent. They share a common logic. They reinforce one another. You may find that as one becomes relevant, others move into the background. Later, the balance may reverse.

That rhythm is expected.

The goal is not familiarity with every model. The goal is coherence.

Frameworks as Reference, Not Instruction

It is important to be clear about what these frameworks are not.

They are not checklists.

They are not prescriptions.

They do not tell you what to do next.

If you are looking for steps, targets, or tactics, you will likely find them incomplete. That incompleteness is deliberate. Tactics age quickly. Context changes. Advice expires.

Frameworks operate at a different level.

They help you see where imbalance is emerging. Where friction is accumulating. Where effort is no longer producing proportional return. They clarify *where* to look before telling you *what* to change.

Often, the most valuable contribution of a framework is not action, but restraint. It slows you down just enough to prevent a reaction that would have felt productive and later proven costly.

Why These Frameworks Emphasize Systems

Each framework in this Appendix describes a system rather than a single variable.

Systems matter because life compounds.

Outcomes are rarely driven by one decision or one habit. They emerge from interactions between energy and judgment, between structure and behavior, between continuity and interruption. Systems reveal those interactions.

When systems are poorly designed, effort leaks. When systems are aligned, progress compounds, often without drama.

The frameworks here are meant to surface those system dynamics early, while correction is still possible and inexpensive.

Embedded, Then Expanded

Many of the frameworks in this Appendix appear, often briefly, within the main body of the book.

That is intentional.

In the narrative, they appear in motion, alongside experience and reflection. In the Appendix, they are gathered, expanded, and made explicit. The two sections serve different cognitive purposes.

If a framework feels familiar, that familiarity is by design. Understanding deepens through exposure, not explanation. The Appendix is not introducing something new so much as giving structure to something already encountered.

Simple Does Not Mean Small

Several of the frameworks in this Appendix are visually spare. Some can be sketched on a single page. That simplicity can be misleading.

A framework's power is not proportional to its complexity. In fact, the opposite is often true. What survives over long horizons is what can be remembered, carried, and applied without constant effort.

Simple structures have fewer failure points. They are easier to return to under stress. They remain usable when attention is limited and circumstances are imperfect.

The frameworks here are intentionally compact so they can travel with you.

How Frameworks Change Over Time

The way you use these frameworks will evolve.

Early on, they may feel aspirational. They describe systems you have not yet fully built. Later, they may feel diagnostic. They reveal drift, imbalance, or areas that need attention.

At different stages of life, different frameworks will matter more. That is not inconsistency. It is responsiveness. A framework that matters deeply in one decade may recede in another, only to return later with new relevance.

The Appendix is designed to accommodate that evolution.

The Role of Judgment

No framework replaces judgment.

A framework cannot tell you when to push or when to pause. It cannot account for every constraint, obligation, or trade-off. It provides orientation, not certainty.

Used poorly, frameworks can become rigid. Used well, they sharpen discretion.

If you find yourself trying to optimize every element of a framework, pause. That impulse usually signals a loss of the larger system. The long game favors alignment over intensity, consistency over novelty, and durability over speed.

Frameworks are meant to inform judgment, not override it.

When to Return to These Pages

The best time to return to a framework is not when things are going well. It is when something feels subtly off.

When progress stalls despite effort.

When complexity creeps in without clear benefit.

When fatigue accumulates without explanation.

When decisions begin to feel urgent rather than considered.

These are not personal failures, but system signals. The frameworks are here to help you read those signals and respond with proportion rather than force.

How Frameworks Are Meant to Function

Used well, a framework becomes a steady companion.

It sits in the background of decisions about work, health, money, and time. It shapes direction without demanding attention. It reduces the need for constant optimization by reinforcing first principles.

You may go months or years without actively thinking about a particular framework. Then, at the right moment, it will surface naturally, offering clarity without noise.

That is the intended relationship.

A Note on Tone and Restraint

This Appendix is intentionally understated.

The frameworks do not attempt to persuade through urgency or performance. They do not rely on novelty, fear, or promise. They assume a reader who is willing to think in decades rather than quarters.

The long game does not reward speed. It rewards continuity. These frameworks are designed accordingly.

What Follows

What follows is not a curriculum to be mastered, nor a system to be implemented all at once. It is a reference—a set of lenses you can return to when something feels misaligned, a way to name patterns before they compound, a structure that supports judgment rather than replacing it.

Used lightly, these frameworks will outlast more elaborate systems. Used patiently, they will compound alongside the life they are meant to support.

That is their role: to serve you not immediately or dramatically, but repeatedly.

THE THREE ENGINES OF A LONG LIFE

This framework is the structural foundation of the long game. It describes how a durable, meaningful life is built not through intensity, optimization, or singular focus, but through the long-term interaction of three reinforcing forms of capacity: intellect, capital, and vitality.

The model is deliberately simple. Its purpose is not to impress, but to orient. Over long horizons, complexity obscures more than it reveals. What compounds is consistency, not brilliance. What breaks down is rarely effort. It's imbalance.

This framework exists to make imbalance visible early, while it is still correctable.

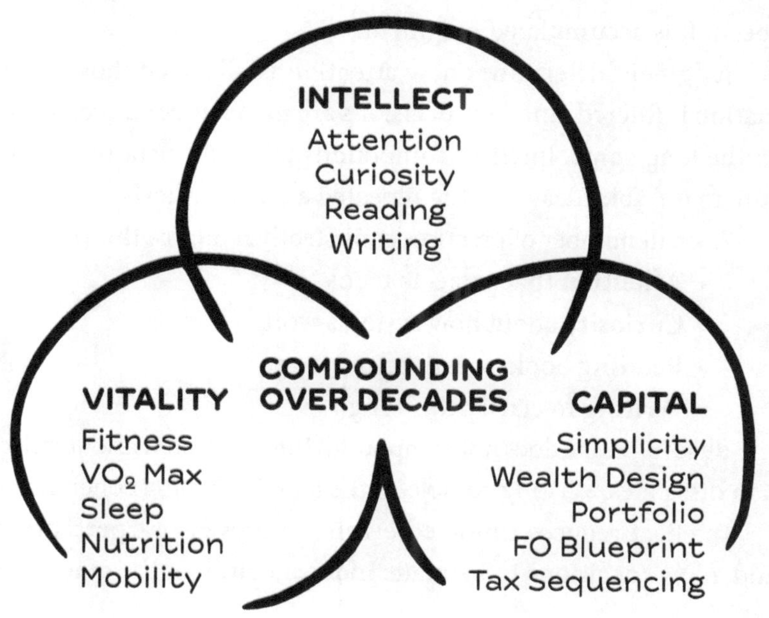

Overview

The long game rejects the idea that life should be optimized in phases. Learn first, earn later. Get fit after success. Reflect once there is time.

That sequencing rarely works.

In reality, each pillar strengthens or weakens the others continuously. Vitality sharpens judgment. Judgment improves capital allocation. Capital protects time, health, and attention. Over decades, the interaction matters more than any individual effort.

Most people pursue these domains sequentially. The long game insists they be cultivated together, imperfectly but persistently.

Each pillar plays a distinct role. Intellect governs judgment. Capital governs optionality. Vitality governs capacity. Together, they determine how decisions compound.

Intellect: Judgement Over Time

Intellect in this framework is not raw intelligence, credentials, or speed. It is accumulated judgment.

Judgment determines how attention is allocated, how information is filtered, and how decisions are made under uncertainty. In the long game, intellect compounds through sustained exposure to durable ideas and the repeated act of synthesis.

A small number of practices consistently reinforce this process:

- **Attention** that protects focus
- **Curiosity** about how systems work
- **Reading** books worth returning to
- **Writing** to clarify thinking

Reading alone does not compound. Information without reflection dissipates. Writing completes the loop by forcing coherence.

Intellect reduces unforced errors, improves risk perception, and allows decisions to be made independently of the emotional cycles of the crowd. Most importantly, it lengthens time horizons.

Without intellect, capital is misallocated and vitality is misdirected. With it, both gain leverage.

Capital: Optionality Without Urgency

Capital in the long game is not about accumulation for its own sake. It is about optionality, the ability to choose without urgency.

Well-designed capital extends time horizons. It allows decisions to be made patiently and without desperation. Poorly designed capital introduces noise, stress, and fragility.

Capital compounds through a restrained set of principles:

- **Simplicity** that preserves freedom
- **Wealth design** aligned with life intent
- **Portfolio discipline** across cycles
- **Tax awareness** that reduces friction

The emphasis is not on maximizing returns, but on avoiding catastrophic loss and unnecessary constraint. When aligned with intellect, capital reinforces clarity. When aligned with vitality, it protects recovery, sleep, and autonomy.

The goal is not excess. The goal is resilience.

Vitality: Capacity That Endures

Vitality is the most underestimated pillar and the first to be sacrificed.

In the long game, vitality is not aesthetic, recreational, or performative. It is strategic infrastructure. Without it, the other pillars decay.

Vitality compounds when the body is treated as a long-lived asset rather than something to be spent. This includes maintaining strength and cardiovascular capacity, preserving mobility, prioritizing sleep, and supporting recovery through nutrition.

At a systems level, vitality is reinforced through:

- **Fitness** for strength and endurance
- **VO₂ Max** as long-term capacity
- **Sleep** as a foundation
- **Nutrition and recovery** for energy
- **Mobility** for resilience

Vitality sharpens thinking, improves emotional regulation, and reduces cognitive noise. Without vitality, intellect dulls and capital loses meaning. With it, both gain longevity.

The Reinforcing Loop

Vitality supports clear thinking. Clear thinking improves capital allocation. Capital protects time, attention, and health.

Over decades, this loop compounds often invisibly, until divergence becomes unmistakable. Decline in one pillar accelerates decline in the others. Strength in one reinforces strength elsewhere.

This is why imbalance matters.

Common Failure Modes

Most people do not abandon the long game intentionally. They drift out of it gradually, often while believing they are still making reasonable choices. Failure in this framework is rarely dramatic. It is slow, cumulative, and easy to rationalize.

Intellect without vitality is an early and common breakdown. Judgment remains sharp, but energy declines. Recovery slows. Attention shortens. Thinking becomes increasingly abstract and less connected to execution. Insight persists, but agency erodes.

Capital without intellect often looks like success until it does not. Wealth grows faster than judgment. Complexity accumulates. Risk is misunderstood or outsourced. Decisions are made emotionally during stress and rationalized afterward. Capital stops compounding and begins to leak through unforced errors.

Vitality without capital creates strength without runway. Health is maintained but not protected. Financial pressure shortens time horizons and introduces stress that undermines recovery. Vitality becomes something that must be defended rather than supported.

Capital without vitality is among the most irreversible failure modes. Financial independence arrives, but physical capacity has already declined. Time exists, but energy does not. Optionality arrives after mobility has narrowed.

Sequential thinking undermines compounding itself. Deferring any pillar introduces opportunity cost that cannot be recovered. The long game requires continuity, not phases.

Optimization without coherence is a distinctly modern failure. Metrics multiply, tracking replaces judgment, and performance crowds out purpose. The system loses its center.

These breakdowns are rarely obvious in real time. They become clear only in retrospect, when divergence has already compounded.

Applying the Model

This framework is not theoretical. It is practical.

Friction in life, fatigue, anxiety, loss of focus, stalled progress, can usually be traced to imbalance within this model. These are system signals, not personal failures.

Return to this framework often. Use it to audit decisions, redesign routines, and extend time horizons. Over decades, small corrections here produce disproportionate results.

THE GEOMETRY OF EXPOSURE

This framework introduces a structural lens for evaluating how decisions compound across time. It does not ask how fast progress is being made. It asks how exposed that progress is to stress.

Effort alone does not determine long-term outcome. Geometry does.

Across decades, lives tend to follow one of three payoff shapes: linear, fragile, or convex.

The purpose of this framework is not prediction. It is early detection.

It exists to make hidden exposure visible while correction is still possible.

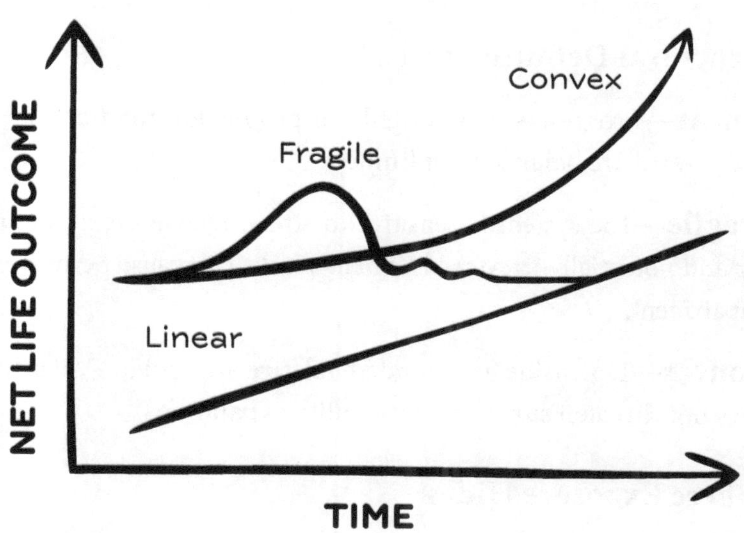

Overview

In the short term, different life trajectories can look similar. Careers advance. Capital accumulates. Health improves. Momentum builds.

The divergence appears later, often only after volatility reveals underlying structure.

A linear path produces proportional outcomes. Progress is steady, and mistakes are usually survivable. The tradeoff is bounded upside. Growth tends to plateau.

A fragile path often accelerates early. Leverage, visibility, or intensity amplify results. But fragility is not about fluctuation; it is about irreversible loss. When tested, fragile systems reset from a lower base. The damage compounds.

A convex path constrains downside while allowing upside to accumulate. Mistakes are survivable. Gains are preserved. Volatility strengthens rather than erodes the system.

The distinction is subtle early and decisive later.

Structural Definitions

Linear—Progress scales roughly in proportion to effort. Risk and reward are balanced but limited.

Fragile—The system is sensitive to stress. Downside is nonlinear and potentially irreversible. Small shocks can cause permanent impairment.

Convex—Downside is bounded relative to upside. Volatility does not threaten survival. Optionality expands.

Where Exposure Hides

Exposure concentrates in three areas:

Intellect becomes fragile when identity fuses with conclusion.

When being right matters more than being accurate. Rigidity replaces curiosity.

Capital becomes fragile when leverage exceeds margin, when lifestyle expands faster than resilience, or when complexity outruns understanding.

Vitality becomes fragile through deferred recovery, chronic sleep compromise, and the slow erosion of physical capacity.

In each domain, fragility rarely feels reckless. It feels justified.

Common Failure Modes

Most breakdowns are gradual.

- Linear effort mistaken for durability
- Leverage introduced during prosperity
- Identity concentrated in role or income
- Vitality deferred in favor of productivity
- Complexity layered without structural review

Fragility compounds quietly until stress reveals it. Convexity, by contrast, is built through margin, restraint, and subtraction. It is less visible early and more powerful later.

Applying the Model

This model is diagnostic.

When progress stalls, examine exposure.

When volatility increases, examine margin.

Before optimizing for growth, examine survivability.

The long game is not about steepening the curve in the present. It is about shaping the curve so that time strengthens rather than erodes it.

Compounding works only when the system survives its own stress.

THE THINKING LOOP

This framework captures how insight compounds. It explains why some people continue to refine judgment year after year, while others accumulate information without ever deepening understanding.

Most people encounter ideas once and move on. The long game depends on returning. Insight compounds only when thinking moves in cycles. Each pass through the loop sharpens the next.

Nothing here is complicated. That is the point. The long game is built not on volume, but on repetition.

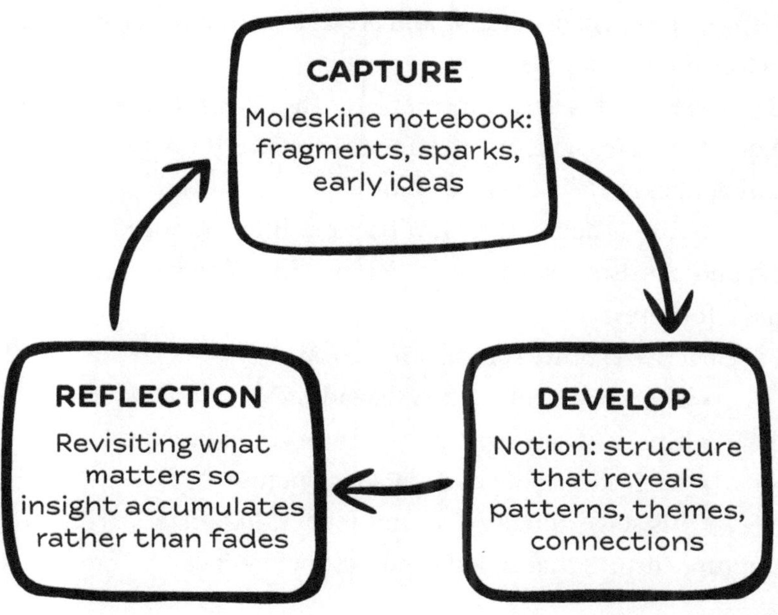

Overview

The Thinking Loop is a simple, continuous cycle: capture, develop, reflect.

Capture strengthens awareness. Development reveals structure. Reflection distills meaning. When the loop runs consistently, insight does not fade. It accumulates.

Most people treat thinking as linear. Read, decide, move on. In the long game, thinking is cyclical. Ideas are revisited, patterns begin to emerge, and understanding deepens.

The loop is not about productivity. It is about compounding judgment.

Each stage serves a distinct function. Capture preserves signal, development reveals structure, and reflection determines what endures. Together, they turn experience into judgment.

Capture: Preserve Signal

Capture is the act of noticing and preserving fragments of thought before they disappear.

Most insights arrive incomplete. They surface as a sentence, a question, a tension, or a fleeting realization. If they are not captured quickly, they are usually lost.

Capture is deliberately low friction. It favors speed over polish and consistency over organization. The goal is not completeness. It is preservation.

Effective capture typically includes:

- Short notes taken during reading
- Observations sparked by conversation or experience
- Early ideas not yet ready for structure

At this stage, quality does not matter. Judgment comes later. Capture ensures that signal is not lost before it can be examined.

Develop: Reveal Structure

Development is where raw material begins to take shape.

This stage involves working with captured ideas long enough to reveal structure. Writing, outlining, or diagramming forces clarity. Weak ideas collapse quickly. Durable ones become clearer with effort.

Development is not about producing finished work. Most development remains private. Its purpose is integration, not output. Development creates:

- Coherent arguments
- Reusable frameworks
- Personal heuristics

Development turns fragments into form. It is where thinking earns its edges.

Reflect: Determining What Endure

Reflection determines what lasts.

This stage involves returning to developed material after time has passed and asking whether it still matters. Many ideas do not. They were momentary or context-specific. Letting them go sharpens judgment.

Reflection is an act of subtraction. It distills meaning by removing what does not endure.

Through reflection, insight accumulates rather than fading. Ideas are no longer tied to the moment they were captured. They become part of a growing internal library.

Without reflection, development becomes noise. With it, understanding deepens.

The Reinforcing Loop

Each stage strengthens the others.

Capture improves as judgment improves. Development becomes faster as structure becomes familiar. Reflection becomes sharper as standards rise.

The loop feeds itself. Clearer thinking leads to better noticing. Better noticing leads to better material. The mind becomes more selective, not more cluttered.

This is how insight compounds.

Common Failure Modes

The most common failure is capture without return. Notes accumulate, but meaning doesn't. The cycle stalls before it ever really starts.

Another failure is development without reflection. Ideas are structured too quickly and never revisited. They feel complete, but they age poorly.

Some people reflect endlessly without developing. Insight feels present but remains vague. Without structure, understanding never solidifies.

The most subtle failure is overengineering. Tools multiply. Systems become elaborate. The loop begins to serve itself rather than insight.

When the loop feels heavy, it stops running. The Thinking Loop works only when it remains simple.

Applying the Model

This framework is not about producing more. It is about retaining more.

If your thinking feels scattered, if insights fade quickly, or if reading no longer translates into clarity, the loop has likely broken down.

Return to the cycle when it's useful. Capture lightly, develop patiently, and reflect honestly.

Over decades, repeated passes through this loop compound into something rare: durable judgment.

THE TWO HALVES OF WEALTH

Wealth is often spoken about as a destination. In practice, it is a condition that must be both created and preserved. These are related skills, but they are not the same skill.

Many people spend years learning how to accumulate assets without ever learning how to protect them. Others become so focused on preservation that they never meaningfully build. Both paths lead to fragility. The long game requires fluency in both halves.

This framework exists to make that distinction explicit. Wealth is not one discipline practiced continuously. It is two disciplines practiced at different moments, often with opposing instincts. One rewards ambition. The other demands restraint.

The Two Halves of Wealth

BECOMING	STAYING
• Live below your means	• Maintain a buffer
• Stay patient and disciplined	• Simplify your finances
• Avoid unnecessary risks	• Protect your independence

Overview

The two halves of wealth are simple, but they are not symmetrical.

Becoming wealthy is an act of construction. It requires forward motion, tolerance for delayed gratification, and the willingness to live differently from those around you. It is additive. Progress is visible.

Staying wealthy is an act of defense. It requires judgment, humility, and the ability to say no long after saying yes was rewarded. It is subtractive. Success is often invisible because disasters never occur.

Most people instinctively favor one half. The long game requires both.

Becoming Wealthy: Building the Foundation

Becoming wealthy begins with margin.

Living below your means is not an accounting exercise. It is a behavioral stance. It requires resisting the gravitational pull of social comparison and opting out of lifestyle escalation before it becomes automatic.

This phase rewards patience. It rewards consistency. It favors simple decisions repeated over long periods rather than clever ones made occasionally.

Becoming wealthy is reinforced through a small number of durable behaviors:

- Maintaining a persistent gap between income and spending
- Building skills that increase earning power
- Investing consistently in broad, productive assets
- Avoiding unnecessary risk that can permanently impair progress

These habits are rarely impressive in the moment. They do not signal status. They do not provide instant feedback. But they create momentum that compounds.

For younger investors, this phase is dominant. The greatest advantage available early is not optimization, but direction. Small, steady decisions establish a base that later choices can build upon.

The danger in this phase is impatience. Chasing shortcuts introduces risk before resilience exists. Becoming wealthy is not about speed. It is about survivability long enough for compounding to matter.

Staying Wealthy: Protecting the Structure

Staying wealthy begins when accumulation is no longer the primary constraint.

At this stage, the risk profile changes. Losses matter more than gains. Complexity becomes dangerous. Emotional decisions carry higher stakes because there is more to protect.

This phase rewards restraint. It rewards clarity. It rewards the ability to distinguish between what is necessary and what is merely available.

Staying wealthy is reinforced through a different set of behaviors:

- Maintaining buffers that absorb unexpected shocks
- Simplifying finances to reduce cognitive and operational risk
- Avoiding obligations that narrow future freedom
- Designing systems that limit emotional decision-making

In this phase, avoiding mistakes matters more than pursuing upside. The most damaging outcomes rarely come from market returns alone. They come from leverage, illiquidity, overconfidence, and lifestyle commitments that cannot flex under stress.

For those in midlife, this phase becomes increasingly important. Careers peak. Responsibilities multiply. Spending often accelerates without intention. The margin for error narrows.

Here, restraint becomes more valuable than ambition. Stability carries more weight than spectacle. Protection becomes a form of progress.

Why the Transition Is Difficult

The shift from becoming wealthy to staying wealthy is psychologically challenging because the instincts conflict.

What worked earlier, taking risk, pushing forward, expanding commitments, can become liabilities later. Many fail to adjust because their identity remains tied to accumulation.

Others overcorrect, retreating into excessive conservatism before the foundation is secure. They protect too early and stagnate.

The long game requires recognizing when the primary challenge has changed. This does not happen on a calendar. It happens when the cost of loss begins to outweigh the benefit of additional gain.

This transition is rarely explicit. It must be recognized deliberately.

Common Failure Modes

One common failure is mastering accumulation while neglecting protection. Wealth grows, but complexity and risk grow faster. A single poor decision can undo decades of progress.

Another failure is confusing wealth with spending capacity. As income rises, lifestyle expands unconsciously. Fixed obligations replace optional ones. Flexibility disappears.

Some focus exclusively on staying wealthy before they have

built enough. Fear replaces patience. Opportunity cost compounds in the background.

There is also the failure of outsourcing judgment. Delegating decisions without understanding the system increases fragility rather than reducing it.

In most cases, failure does not arrive dramatically. It arrives through drift.

Applying the Model

This framework is not about choosing one half over the other. It is about knowing which discipline deserves emphasis now.

If progress feels stalled early, examine whether protection has arrived too soon. If stress increases later, examine whether ambition has overstayed its usefulness.

Return to this model during transitions. Career changes. Windfalls. Lifestyle shifts. These moments often require rebalancing between the two halves.

Over decades, wealth endures less because returns are extraordinary and more because behavior stays aligned with the phase you're in. Becoming wealthy builds the structure. Staying wealthy preserves it.

THE POWER OF A SIMPLE PORTFOLIO

This framework distills the portfolio architecture introduced earlier into a reusable system. It is not about security selection, market timing, or tactical optimization. It is about structure. Specifically, how to design a portfolio that compounds quietly in the background while protecting decision quality through volatility, uncertainty, and time.

The purpose of this framework is recall. It exists to make the architecture visible again when emotion, noise, or complexity begin to creep in.

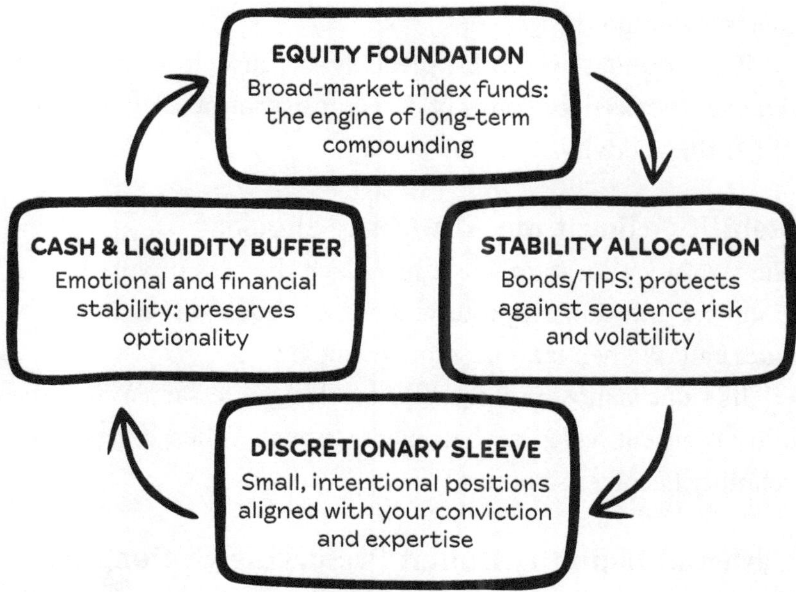

Overview

A portfolio designed for a lifetime must do more than generate returns. It must support behavior. That requires a structure that can compound, absorb shocks, preserve flexibility, and allow limited expression without threatening the foundation.

Each component in this framework serves a specific function. None is designed to stand alone. Together, they create a structure that compounds steadily and can be held through cycles rather than reacted to during them.

Components
Equity Foundation: Compounding the Core

The equity foundation exists to capture long-term economic growth. Broad, diversified exposure does the heavy lifting over decades. Its role is not to be exciting, adaptive, or expressive. Its role is to compound.

This foundation works precisely because it is boring. It removes the need for constant decision-making and allows time, rather than activity, to do the work.

Stability Allocation: Absorbing Shocks

The stability allocation exists to reduce the cost of volatility. It dampens drawdowns, protects against sequence risk, and provides ballast when markets reprice quickly.

Its value is most visible when it feels unnecessary. When stability is absent, volatility becomes personal. When it is present, volatility becomes structural.

Cash and Liquidity Buffer: Preserving Optionality

Liquidity exists to protect decision quality. Cash reduces the likelihood of forced selling, creates flexibility during stress, and stabilizes behavior when uncertainty rises.

This component is not idle. It preserves optionality and protects the portfolio from becoming brittle at exactly the wrong moment.

Discretionary Sleeve: Thoughtful Expression

The discretionary sleeve exists to allow limited expression without undermining discipline. These positions are intentionally small. Their purpose is not to drive outcomes, but to satisfy curiosity, conviction, or expertise while keeping the core intact.

When sized correctly, discretion relieves pressure elsewhere in the system. When oversized, it becomes the primary source of fragility.

The Reinforcing Structure

When these elements work together, the portfolio becomes more than a collection of holdings. It becomes a system.

The equity foundation compounds in the background. Stability reduces the emotional cost of volatility. Liquidity prevents forced decisions. Discretion allows expression without jeopardizing the whole.

No single component is asked to do everything. That is the source of the system's strength.

Common Failure Modes

Most portfolio failures are not analytical. They are structural.

Complexity is often mistaken for sophistication. As complexity increases, clarity declines and conviction weakens. Discretion grows too large. Stability is removed to chase marginal return. Liquidity is minimized in the name of efficiency.

The portfolio becomes harder to understand and harder to hold. Volatility feels personal. Decisions accelerate. The system begins reacting instead of compounding.

The most common breakdown occurs when discretion overwhelms structure. The second is when liquidity is ignored until it is urgently needed. In both cases, the failure is not market-driven. It is design-driven.

Applying the Model

Use this framework to audit whether your portfolio supports long-term behavior.

If staying invested feels difficult, the issue is usually structural rather than informational. Small adjustments to design often matter more than changes in allocation.

A portfolio that wins is not one that looks impressive on a spreadsheet. It is one that can be held through noise, through cycles, and through the changing seasons of your own life.

THE FOUR PILLARS OF STEWARDSHIP

As wealth grows, clarity becomes more valuable than cleverness.

Most financial stress at higher levels of net worth does not come from lack of opportunity. It comes from fragmentation. Decisions get made one at a time, without stepping back to see the whole. Accounts slowly pile up. Commitments layer on. Before long, you're responding to what's in front of you instead of choosing with intention.

The Four Pillars of Stewardship exist to prevent that outcome. They provide structure without creating complexity. They reduce the need for constant reevaluation. They allow wealth to support life rather than demanding attention.

This is not bureaucracy. It is design.

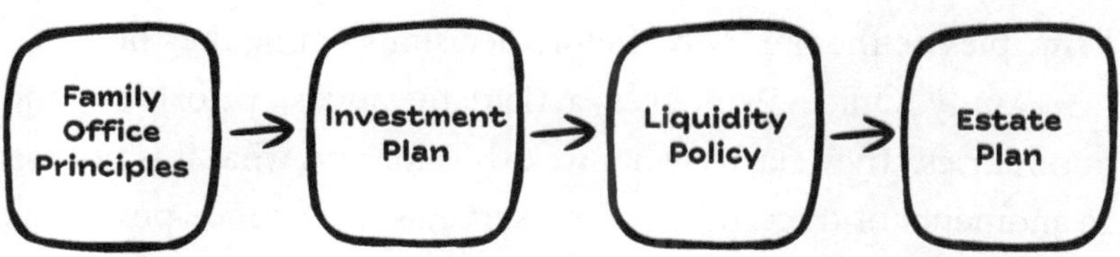

Overview

Stewardship begins when accumulation is no longer the primary challenge.

At this stage, the question shifts from "How do I grow?" to "How do I remain aligned?" Wealth starts to feel less one-dimensional. Investments carry stories and context. Liquidity isn't just a number on a statement, it represents flexibility and choice. Taxes are no longer theoretical. And legacy shifts from a distant idea to something that asks for care and responsibility.

Without structure, these domains compete for attention. They introduce noise. They create friction. They increase the likelihood of reactive decisions made under stress.

The Four Pillars provide a rhythm for financial life. They create a posture of calm oversight rather than constant monitoring. Each pillar serves a distinct role. Together, they form a coherent system that scales with complexity instead of being overwhelmed by it.

Family Office Principles: Anchoring Intent

Principles define the "why" before decisions define the "how."

Family Office Principles articulate values, priorities, and boundaries. They clarify what wealth is for and what it is not for. In moments of uncertainty, they serve as a reference point that prevents drift.

This pillar is not about control. It is about continuity. It ensures that decisions remain aligned with the person you are becoming rather than the emotions of the moment.

Without principles, every decision feels open-ended. With them, many decisions resolve themselves.

Investment Plan: Providing Direction

The Investment Plan translates intent into action.

It defines asset allocation, risk tolerance, and decision rules. It removes the need to reinvent strategy during periods of market stress. When volatility rises, the plan absorbs emotion before it reaches behavior.

This pillar is not designed to optimize returns. It is designed to preserve discipline across cycles. It allows compounding to occur in the background without constant intervention.

Without an explicit plan, judgment is outsourced to headlines and sentiment. With one, behavior remains steady even when conditions are not.

Liquidity Policy: Preserving Flexibility

Liquidity is not idle capital. It is insurance for decision quality.

A Liquidity Policy defines how much flexibility the system requires to remain resilient. It prevents forced selling. It allows opportunity to be evaluated calmly rather than seized urgently.

This pillar reduces fragility. It ensures that temporary disruptions do not become permanent mistakes. It protects optionality precisely when it is most valuable.

Without a liquidity framework, stress becomes personal. With one, stress becomes structural.

Estate Plan: Extending Stewardship

The Estate Plan addresses continuity beyond the present.

It clarifies how assets are transferred, governed, and protected. It reduces uncertainty for those who will inherit responsibility rather than merely benefit. It ensures that intent survives transitions.

This pillar is not about mortality. It is about order. It transforms wealth from something that ends into something that continues with purpose.

Without an estate framework, complexity is deferred rather than resolved. With one, legacy becomes deliberate rather than accidental.

The System Effect

Individually, each pillar provides stability. Together, they create coherence.

Principles guide the plan. The plan informs liquidity needs. Liquidity supports discipline. The estate structure ensures continuity. Decisions stop occurring in isolation and begin flowing from a unified system.

When these pillars are in place, financial life becomes quieter. Fewer decisions feel urgent. Fewer situations require improvisation. The system carries weight, so the individual does not have to.

This is the difference between managing wealth and stewarding it.

Capacity Across the Life Arc

Early in life, adopting this mindset creates leverage.

A simplified version of these pillars teaches intention before complexity arrives. Small systems built early compound in effectiveness as wealth grows. Stewardship becomes natural rather than corrective.

Later in life, the framework becomes essential.

As responsibilities expand, structure prevents overload. Investments, property, income planning, and taxes stop competing for attention. They are integrated. The system scales without becoming brittle.

The micro family office mindset transforms noise into order.

Common Failure Modes

One failure is delaying structure until complexity feels overwhelming. By then, decisions have already become reactive. Another is overengineering. Excess documentation creates friction rather than clarity. The purpose is alignment, not administration.

Some rely on instinct alone, assuming experience substitutes for structure. This increases emotional decision-making rather than reducing it. There is also the failure of rigidity. Principles and plans must evolve as life changes. Stewardship requires adjustment without abandonment.

Applying the Model

This framework is not something you put in place and walk away from. It is something you return to when life shifts.

Transitions are usually the signal. A change in career. An unexpected gain. A difficult market. A change within the family. These are the moments that reveal whether your structure is actually guiding behavior or simply sitting on paper.

When decisions start to feel urgent or unsettled, step back. Revisit the pillars. Clarify what you are trying to protect and what you are trying to build. Make sure liquidity still gives you flexibility. Make sure continuity still holds.

Practiced consistently, this approach changes the role wealth plays in your life. It moves from something that demands constant attention to something that supports you.

That is stewardship.

THE ARCHITECTURE
OF LIFETIME INCOME

Income stacking is a sequencing problem, not an optimization problem. The question is not how much income to generate at once, but how different sources arrive, overlap, and recede across a lifetime. When income is designed as a system rather than a collection of streams, it becomes more resilient, more flexible, and far easier to live with.

The purpose of this model is orientation. It exists to make the order of operations visible before transitions arrive and decisions become reactive. Actual timing of each source will vary—the graph is for illustrative purposes only.

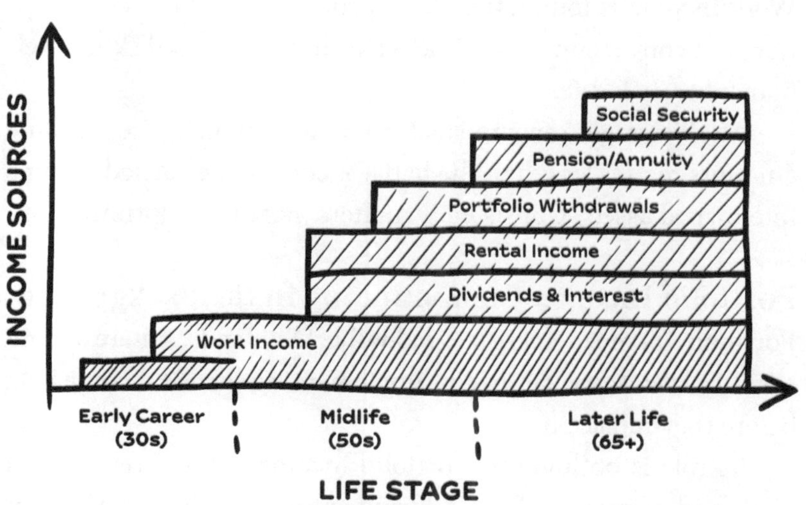

Overview

Different sources of income become useful at different stages of life. Some appear early and fade. Others arrive later and persist. Very few switch on or off cleanly.

When designed well, income sources overlap intentionally. Those overlaps smooth transitions, reduce dependence on any single stream, and preserve flexibility as circumstances change. When designed poorly, income becomes brittle, timing-dependent, and emotionally charged.

This model focuses on sequencing rather than scale.

Each income layer serves a distinct purpose. Early income builds assets. Midlife income broadens stability. Later income sustains independence. Together, they form a system that supports choice rather than urgency.

Core Income Layers
Work Income: Building the Base

Work income is foundational. Its primary role is not consumption, but conversion. It funds asset accumulation and skill development early in life.

At this stage, income stacking is directional. The absolute amounts matter less than the habit of converting earned income into owned assets. Consistency matters more than optimization.

Portfolio Income: Compounding in the Background

Portfolio income emerges gradually. Dividends, interest, and eventually withdrawals begin supplementing earned income long before they replace it.

Its role is optionality. Portfolio income reduces reliance on work and creates flexibility during transitions. The goal is not acceleration, but maturation.

Rental or Business Income: Diversifying Cash Flow

Rental or business income introduces a different risk profile. It is often less passive, but more controllable. When sized appropriately, it reduces reliance on market-driven income alone.

This layer adds resilience, not complexity. It should support the system, not dominate it.

Pension or Annuity Income: Stabilizing the Floor

Guaranteed income provides structural stability later in life. Its purpose is predictability rather than growth.

This layer reduces sequence risk and anchors baseline expenses. When present, it allows other assets to remain invested longer and with greater confidence.

Social Security: Inflation-Linked Longevity Protection

Social Security functions as delayed insurance. Its value increases with patience and longevity.

This layer is not meant to be optimized tactically. It is meant to arrive when other income sources are most exposed to longevity risk.

The Reinforcing Structure

Income stacking works because no single source is asked to do everything.

Work income builds assets. Assets generate portfolio income. Portfolio income bridges transitions. Guaranteed income stabilizes later life. Social Security protects against outliving the system.

The strength lies in overlap. Each layer arrives before it is strictly necessary and remains useful longer than expected.

Common Failure Modes

The most common failure is attempting to activate every income source at once. This creates complexity without resilience.

Another failure is waiting too long to introduce diversification. Overreliance on a single income stream increases fragility and forces reactive decisions when conditions change.

A subtler failure is ignoring sequencing. Starting guaranteed income too early or drawing on portfolios prematurely shortens the system's lifespan.

Income systems fail not from lack of effort, but from poor order of operations.

Applying the Model

Use this model to evaluate whether your income sources are arriving in the right sequence and overlapping intentionally.

If transitions feel stressful, the issue is usually structural. Small adjustments to timing often matter more than increases in income.

The goal is not to maximize income. It is to design an income system that adapts as life evolves and supports independence across decades.

That is the work this model is meant to guide.

THE QUIET ARBITRAGE
BETWEEN HEALTH AND WEALTH

Over a lifetime, two forms of capital compound on different schedules. Financial capacity tends to expand with time. Physical capacity, unless deliberately protected, tends to contract. The gap between them rarely announces itself, but it quietly determines the range of life available to us.

This model exists to make that gap visible early, while choices still compound and corrections remain gentle.

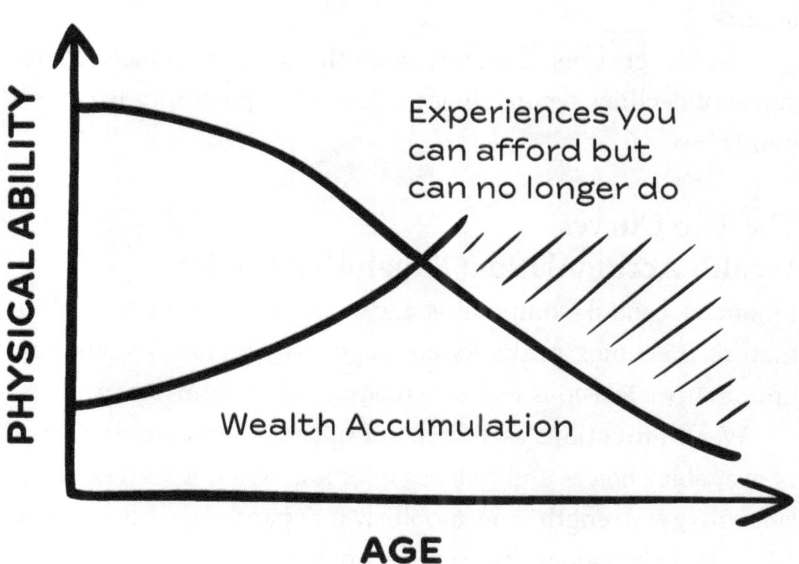

Overview

Wealth and health do not behave symmetrically across decades.

Wealth benefits from patience, leverage, and delayed gratification. Its compounding accelerates later in life, often just as income peaks and accumulated assets begin to work meaningfully in the background. Health behaves differently. Its compounding is front-loaded. Strength, cardiovascular capacity, mobility, and resilience respond best to early and consistent investment.

When these curves move together, wealth expands life. When they diverge, optionality narrows. Experiences remain affordable, but no longer fully accessible. The loss is not financial. It is experiential.

This divergence is rarely dramatic. It unfolds slowly, then all at once.

Health governs capacity. Wealth governs choice. When capacity declines before choice expands, opportunity is permanently lost.

The Two Curves
Wealth Accumulation: Expanding Choice

Financial capital compounds most visibly later in life. Skills mature. Earnings peak. Assets begin to generate income and optionality. Decisions feel less constrained by immediacy.

Wealth functions as a force multiplier. It increases the range of available choices and reduces urgency. When it arrives alongside energy, strength, and mobility, it expands what is possible. When it arrives alone, its power is limited.

Wealth cannot restore time. It can only expand what remains.

Physical Capacity: Shrinking Range

Physical capacity declines by default. Strength erodes. Aerobic capacity diminishes. Mobility narrows. Recovery slows. These changes are gradual and easy to rationalize in the moment.

Early losses feel invisible. Daily function remains intact. Later losses feel irreversible. The range of feasible experiences contracts long before basic health is threatened.

Capacity is not binary. It fades along a slope. By the time its absence is obvious, much of it has already been forfeited.

Why the Gap Widens

The gap widens because incentives are misaligned across time.

Early in life, time feels abundant and resources feel scarce. It is rational to prioritize earning, saving, and deferring gratification. Health investments feel optional because their benefits appear distant and intangible.

Later in life, resources feel more abundant and time feels constrained. Health becomes urgent, but capacity has already begun to decline. Investments made late preserve function, but rarely restore range.

Most people optimize locally within each phase. They behave rationally in isolation, but irrationally across the full arc. The result is a life that compounds wealth effectively while allowing capacity to erode in parallel.

This is not a failure of discipline. It is a failure of timing.

The Arbitrage

The arbitrage exists in asymmetry.

Health invested early preserves capacity later. Wealth accumulated later expands choice only if capacity remains intact. When the two are aligned, wealth redeems time. When they are misaligned, wealth arrives after capacity has already faded.

This is why postponement is so costly. Experiences deferred are often experiences forfeited, even if financial resources eventually become abundant. What is lost is not money, but the ability to fully inhabit what money can make possible.

The arbitrage is quiet because it produces no immediate pain. It reveals itself only in hindsight.

Common Failure Modes

The most common failure is assuming health can be recovered on demand. Financial setbacks often allow recovery. Physical setbacks rarely do. Lost capacity does not compound back.

Another failure is treating health as maintenance rather than infrastructure. Minimal effort preserves basic function but not range. Range is what enables meaningful experience.

A subtler failure is viewing wealth as compensation for decline. Comfort increases, but capability does not. Life becomes easier, but smaller.

The defining feature of these failures is irreversibility. Financial mistakes can often be corrected with time and discipline. Physical decline rarely offers the same symmetry. Once the gap has widened, it cannot be closed with resources alone.

Applying the Model

Use this model to assess whether your investments are aligned across time.

If wealth is compounding while your range of physical experience is narrowing, the imbalance is already forming. The correction is rarely financial.

A useful test is to ask whether your future resources are arriving faster than your future capacity is shrinking. If the answer is unclear, the system is already misaligned.

Corrections made early are modest. Corrections made late are constrained.

Health invested early multiplies the return on wealth later. Wealth built patiently protects the space to invest in health now. Neither can substitute for the other.

The real measure of wealth is not what it accumulates, but the life it allows you to live while capacity still exists.

That is the quiet arbitrage this model is meant to protect.

THE CAPACITY CURVE

Across decades of longevity research, few variables show a relationship to survival as strong, as consistent, or as underappreciated as cardiorespiratory fitness. VO_2 max, a measure of the body's ability to transport and utilize oxygen, functions less like a performance metric and more like a systems-level signal of resilience.

It reflects how efficiently the heart, lungs, blood vessels, and muscles work together under stress. More importantly, it reflects how much margin the system retains as conditions deteriorate.

The Capacity Curve makes this visible: as capacity increases, risk recedes.

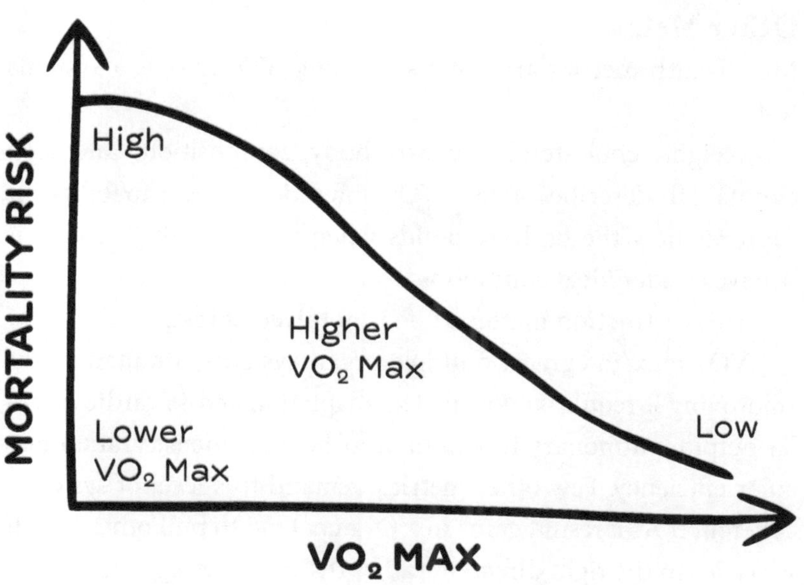

Overview

VO₂ max illustrates a simple truth that many people resist: capacity matters more than appearance.

As VO₂ max rises, mortality risk falls. Not in steps, but along a continuous gradient. There is no single threshold beyond which benefit stops. Each incremental gain improves the system's margin for error.

Most health strategies focus on eliminating negatives. VO₂ max compounds positives. It increases reserve. Reserve is what allows a system to absorb shock without cascading failure.

This is why VO₂ max aligns so closely with the long game. It rewards consistency over intensity, structure over novelty, and patience over urgency. It compounds in the background, much like capital and judgment.

Why VO₂ Max Outperforms Almost Every Other Metric

Most health metrics are static snapshots. VO₂ max is a systems test.

Weight, cholesterol, glucose, body composition, and step counts all describe states. VO₂ max describes capability. It captures how the body responds when pushed, not just how it behaves under ideal conditions.

This distinction matters. Life is not lived at rest.

VO₂ max integrates multiple organ systems simultaneously. Improving it requires coordinated adaptation across cardiovascular output, pulmonary function, mitochondrial density, and muscular efficiency. Few other metrics demand this level of systemic coherence. As a result, gains in VO₂ max tend to pull other health variables in the right direction rather than competing with them.

It also reflects reserve capacity. Two people may share similar labs and outward health markers. The one with higher VO_2 max has greater margin. Margin determines how well the body tolerates illness, injury, stress, and aging itself.

Most people optimize what is visible or easy to track. VO_2 max resists shortcuts. It cannot be meaningfully improved through diet alone or brief interventions. It responds to repeated exposure to controlled stress followed by recovery. That makes it an unusually honest metric.

In a world saturated with health data, VO_2 max remains one of the few measures that reliably reflects how much life the body can support.

Capacity Across the Life Arc

In early adulthood, VO_2 max represents compounded advantage.

Youth amplifies adaptation. Training responses are fast. Habits formed early become defaults rather than interventions. A strong aerobic base built in this season carries forward with surprisingly little maintenance.

This is when endurance is easiest to build and easiest to protect. Establishing a high baseline early sets the trajectory for the decades that follow.

Later in life, VO_2 max becomes something else. It becomes evidence that decline is not inevitable.

Many people assume their best physical capacity is behind them. Yet the science is clear. VO_2 max can rise at any age. It responds to structure and consistency, not nostalgia. Improvements in midlife and beyond meaningfully reduce mortality risk and preserve functional independence.

In this sense, VO_2 max becomes proof that physiology responds to intention, not just time. You can, in a very real way, grow younger from the inside out.

Relationship to The Long Game

This framework connects directly to the quiet arbitrage between health and wealth.

When physical capacity is preserved early, wealth expands what is possible later. Experiences remain available. Energy remains abundant. Time feels open.

When capacity is neglected, wealth often arrives after the window has narrowed. Money increases choice on paper, but the body can no longer fully redeem it.

VO_2 max determines how wide that window remains.

It protects the ability to travel, explore, engage, and recover. It reduces the gap between what resources allow and what the body can still do. In this way, VO_2 max is not merely a health metric. It is a life-capacity metric.

Common Failure Modes

The most common failure is postponement. Fitness is treated as something to return to later, once work stabilizes or responsibilities ease. Later rarely arrives with the same physiological leverage.

Another failure is substitution. Aesthetics, weight loss, or general activity are mistaken for capacity. These can coexist with low cardiorespiratory fitness. VO_2 max declines unless it is trained deliberately.

There is also the failure of overcomplexity. Protocols multiply. Devices accumulate. Metrics crowd out the simple work of sustained cardiovascular stress and recovery. When the system becomes heavy, consistency erodes.

Finally, many abandon endurance work because progress feels slow. VO_2 max compounds gradually. Its gains are often visible only in retrospect. People quit just as the curve begins to bend.

Applying the Model

This framework is not about chasing athletic performance. It is about protecting your range.

When fatigue rises, ambition narrows, stress feels heavier, and recovery slows, something is shifting. These are not character flaws. They are signals. The system is asking for attention.

VO_2 max gives you a practical response. Strengthen the system. Respect recovery. Keep structure in place. Allow adaptation to unfold.

Over the years, the benefits extend well beyond fitness. Higher capacity supports clearer thinking, steadier emotion, and a longer view when decisions matter. It protects your ability to stay fully engaged in the life you are building.

That is why VO_2 max belongs near the foundation of the long game. It does not guarantee longevity. It protects possibility.

THE TIER 1
CIVILIAN PROTOCOL

Durable fitness is not built by chasing peak performance. It is built by designing a body that continues to work as life unfolds.

Strength, endurance, mobility, and core integrity are often trained in isolation or rotated in and out depending on trends, injuries, or motivation. This fragmented approach produces predictable failure. Strength without mobility leads to stiffness and pain. Endurance without strength erodes resilience. Mobility without load becomes fragile. Core work without integration becomes cosmetic.

The Tier 1 Civilian Protocol exists to prevent that drift. It describes fitness as an architecture rather than a collection of exercises. Each component plays a distinct role. None is sufficient on its own. Together, they create a body that remains capable, adaptable, and resilient across decades.

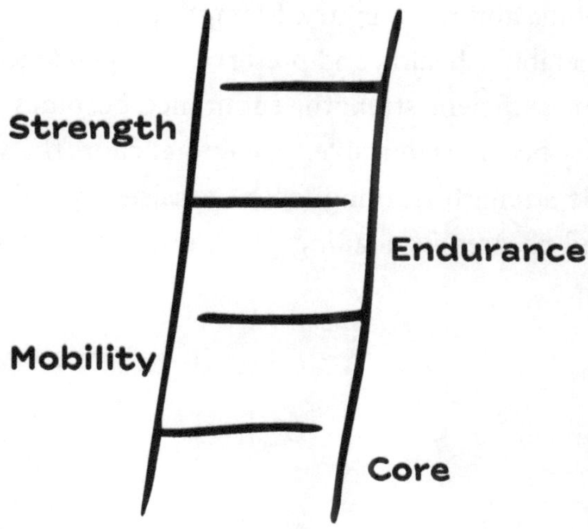

Overview

The Tier 1 Civilian Protocol is built on a simple premise: capacity must be broad to last.

Most people train for what they enjoy or what they are already good at. This narrows the system. Durable fitness moves in the opposite direction. It prioritizes balance over specialization and continuity over intensity.

Strength provides force. Endurance provides energy. Mobility provides range. Core integrity provides transfer and control. When one is neglected, the system compensates. Compensation works for a while. Eventually, it fails.

The long game approach is not to avoid stress, but to distribute it intelligently. This framework exists to ensure that stress strengthens the system rather than breaking it.

Strength: Preserving Force

Strength is the ability to produce force against resistance. It is the most visible component of fitness, but also the most misunderstood.

In the long game, strength is not about maximal lifts or aesthetic outcomes. It is about preserving the ability to move objects, stabilize joints, and resist injury. Strength protects bone density, supports metabolic health, and preserves independence.

Without sufficient strength, endurance becomes inefficient and mobility becomes unstable. Strength anchors the system.

Durable strength training favors consistency, full ranges of motion, and progressive loading. It is meant to support life, not dominate it.

Endurance: Sustaining Capacity

Endurance determines how long the system can perform without degradation.

This component supports cardiovascular health, metabolic flexibility, and recovery capacity. It allows effort to be repeated day after day without accumulating excessive fatigue. Endurance is what keeps activity feeling available rather than costly.

In the context of durable fitness, endurance is not about constant exhaustion. It is about maintaining a wide aerobic base that supports both daily movement and occasional intensity.

Without endurance, strength becomes expensive. Recovery slows. Fatigue accumulates until participation shrinks.

Mobility: Preserving Range

Mobility is the ability to move joints through their intended ranges under control.

It is often confused with flexibility. In reality, mobility reflects usable range, not passive stretch. It determines how well strength and endurance can be expressed without friction.

As people age, mobility is usually the first component to decline and the last to be addressed. This inversion creates pain, compensation, and unnecessary limitation.

Durable fitness treats mobility as a form of maintenance. It keeps the system lubricated, adaptable, and resistant to stiffness-driven injury.

Core Integrity: Transferring Force

The core is not a muscle group. It is a system that transfers force between the upper and lower body.

Core integrity stabilizes movement, protects the spine, and allows strength and endurance to express safely. Without it, power leaks. Compensation increases. Injury risk rises.

In this framework, core work is not isolated or aesthetic. It is functional. It emphasizes control, posture, and coordination under load.

A strong core allows the rest of the system to operate efficiently rather than defensively.

Capacity Across the Life Arc

Early in life, this architecture builds surplus.

Training across all four components creates a wide base of capacity that carries forward even as life becomes more complex. Fitness becomes an identity rather than a project. Decline is delayed not through effort, but through structure.

Later in life, the same architecture becomes restorative.

Strength can be rebuilt without excess joint stress. Endurance can be expanded without chronic fatigue. Mobility can be recovered in ways that reduce pain rather than provoke it. Core integrity restores confidence in movement.

The body responds to intention at any age. What changes is not adaptability, but tolerance for imbalance. This framework exists to preserve balance.

Common Failure Modes

The most common failure is specialization. One component dominates while others decay. The system appears functional until it is tested.

Another failure is episodic training. Intensity spikes followed by long gaps produce fatigue without adaptation. Durable fitness requires continuity.

Some overemphasize endurance at the expense of strength, assuming movement alone is enough. Others pursue strength while ignoring mobility, accumulating stiffness and pain.

Finally, many abandon structure altogether after injury or disruption, assuming decline is inevitable. In reality, injury often signals imbalance rather than age.

Applying the Model

This framework is not a rigid program. It is a way of seeing.

When pain starts to surface, mobility or core stability is often the missing piece. When fatigue lingers, endurance may need attention. When ordinary tasks begin to feel heavier than they should, strength has likely declined. The body usually makes the pattern visible, if you are willing to notice it.

Return to this structure when your training begins to feel scattered or reactive. Use it to recalibrate rather than to overhaul everything at once.

Practiced consistently, this approach protects something more important than peak output. It protects your ability to stay in the game.

COMPOUNDING MOMENTUM
AND THE RESET CYCLE

Progress is not determined by intensity. It is determined by continuity.

Most people believe they are inconsistent because they lack discipline or motivation. In reality, the problem is structural. Their effort is organized in a way that guarantees reset rather than compounding. They work hard, pause, recover, and restart. The cycle repeats. Energy is spent, but capacity does not accumulate.

This framework makes that distinction visible. It contrasts two paths that often look similar in the short term but diverge dramatically over time. One path builds compounding momentum through consistency. The other follows the familiar reset cycle of start, stop, recover, repeat. Both involve effort. Only one produces durable progress.

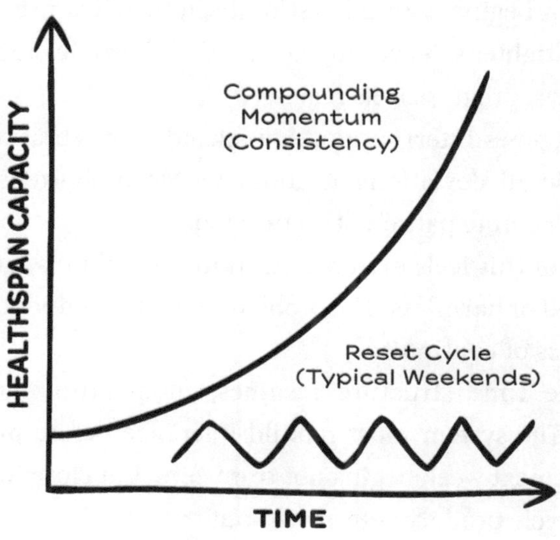

Overview

Compounding momentum is not about doing more. It is about interrupting less.

The reset cycle feels productive because it includes visible effort. Training sessions are hard. Workdays are full. Weeks feel disciplined. The problem is not effort. The problem is interruption. Each reset extracts a tax that is rarely acknowledged.

Momentum builds when inputs remain continuous enough for adaptation to occur. Fitness improves when stress and recovery are repeated without prolonged disruption. Judgment improves when thinking is revisited rather than restarted. Capital compounds when contributions are steady and behavior remains stable across cycles.

The long game favors momentum because it reduces the cost of restarting. The difference between momentum and reset becomes structural rather than motivational.

The Reset Cycle

The reset cycle is familiar because it is socially reinforced.

It often begins with a burst of discipline. Training resumes. Nutrition tightens. Sleep improves. Work becomes focused. For several days, progress feels real.

Then comes interruption. A weekend. A celebration. Travel. Fatigue. Small deviations accumulate. Sleep shortens. Alcohol appears. Training pauses. Structure loosens.

None of this feels extreme. Each interruption is rationalized as deserved or harmless. The problem is not the individual choice. It is the loss of continuity.

By the time structure resumes, momentum has already decayed. The system must rebuild tolerance before progressing again. The next week begins not from zero, but close to it.

This cycle produces effort without trajectory.

Compounding Momentum

Compounding momentum operates differently. It does not eliminate rest, flexibility, or enjoyment. It preserves continuity through them.

Momentum is built when stress, recovery, and behavior remain sufficiently consistent that adaptation compounds rather than resets. Training continues at a lower intensity rather than stopping entirely. Nutrition relaxes without collapsing. Sleep shortens occasionally without becoming chaotic.

The system bends without breaking.

Momentum feels quieter than the reset cycle. There are fewer dramatic swings. Progress is less noticeable day to day. But the underlying capacity curve continues upward.

This is why compounding momentum often goes unnoticed by those living inside it. The work feels sustainable rather than heroic. The payoff appears later.

Where the Reset Cycle Hides

For many people, the reset cycle is most visible on weekends.

A structured week is followed by poorer food choices, disrupted sleep, and alcohol. None of this feels excessive in isolation. But the cumulative effect is interruption. Progress made earlier in the week is partially undone, not through indulgence, but through inconsistency.

The same pattern appears in work. Deep focus during the week gives way to distraction. Reading is replaced by scanning. Writing pauses. Reflection disappears. Monday begins with reacclimation rather than continuation.

In finance, the reset cycle appears as emotional reactions to short-term volatility. Contributions pause. Plans are revisited unnecessarily. Decisions are delayed or reversed. The system loses its steady rhythm.

The reset cycle isn't a willpower problem. It's usually a design problem.

Why Consistency Compounds Disproportionately

Small interruptions carry outsized cost.

Physiological systems adapt through repeated exposure. When exposure stops, adaptation stalls. Restarting requires reacclimation before progress resumes. The same is true cognitively and financially. Each reset consumes time and energy that could have compounded.

Consistency reduces friction. Habits become default rather than effortful. Decision fatigue declines. Recovery becomes predictable. The system spends less energy maintaining itself and more energy adapting upward.

This is why moderate consistency often outperforms sporadic intensity over long horizons. It keeps the curve bending in the right direction.

Common Misconceptions

One misconception is that momentum requires perfection. It does not. It requires continuity.

Another is that rest necessitates stopping. In reality, rest can be active, lighter, or adaptive without being disruptive.

Many believe momentum demands constant discipline. In practice, it reduces the need for discipline by embedding behavior into structure.

There is also the belief that resets are harmless if they are brief. Frequent small resets accumulate into large opportunity cost.

Finally, some confuse novelty with progress. New programs, new tools, and fresh starts feel motivating. But novelty often resets adaptation rather than advancing it.

Relationship to The Long Game

This framework sits beneath many others in the book.

The Thinking Loop compounds insight only when it is revisited. The Tier 1 Civilian Protocol works only when training continues across weeks and seasons. VO_2 max improves through sustained exposure rather than episodic effort. Capital compounds through steady behavior, not bursts of optimization.

Momentum is the connective tissue.

The long game is not about intensity spikes. It is about reducing the number of times you have to start over.

Common Failure Modes

The most common failure is binary thinking. On or off. Disciplined or indulgent. This framing guarantees reset.

Another failure is using recovery as justification for abandonment. True recovery preserves structure while reducing load.

Some people overcorrect after interruption, attempting to regain lost ground through intensity. This often produces injury, burnout, or further reset.

Others misinterpret plateaus as failure and restart unnecessarily. In reality, plateaus are often periods of consolidation before further adaptation.

Applying the Model

The question is not whether interruptions will occur. They will.

The question is whether your system absorbs them or resets because of them.

When progress stalls, examine continuity before increasing effort. Ask where structure disappears. Identify where weekends, travel, or stress introduce full stops rather than gentle bends.

Design for momentum. Lower the floor rather than raising

the ceiling. Preserve minimums. Keep the loop running.

Over decades, this approach produces a quiet but decisive advantage. Capacity accumulates. Effort feels lighter. Progress becomes durable.

THE LONGEVITY PLAYBOOK

Longevity is often framed as avoidance. Avoid disease. Avoid injury. Avoid decline. That framing misses the point.

A long life worth inhabiting is not sustained by avoidance alone. It is sustained by a system that reinforces capacity, clarity, and engagement. The Longevity Playbook exists to describe that system.

Rather than treating health behaviors as separate domains to be optimized independently, this framework shows how a small set of foundational elements interact. When aligned, they reduce friction rather than adding effort. They form a loop that compounds vitality instead of draining it.

This isn't just a routine. It's intentional design.

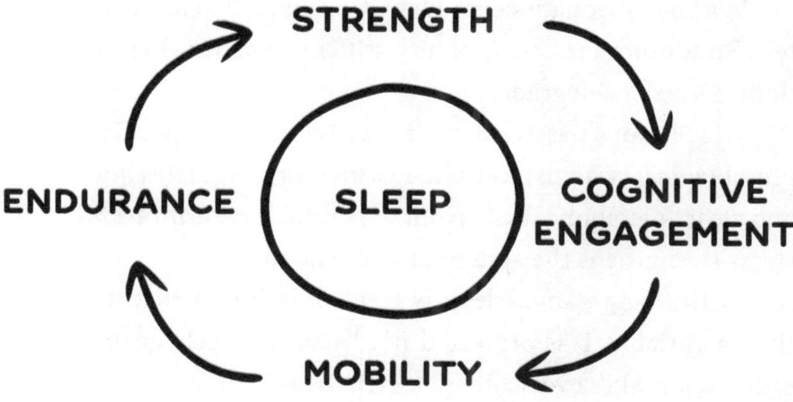

Overview

Most people approach longevity by accumulating tactics. Supplements are added. Workouts are changed. Sleep is addressed sporadically. Cognitive health is discussed abstractly.

The issue isn't effort. It's how scattered it becomes.

The Longevity Playbook begins with a different assumption: vitality is sustained by coherence. When core elements are aligned, the system becomes self-reinforcing. When they are misaligned, even disciplined effort produces diminishing returns.

At the center of this system is sleep. Around it sit strength, endurance, mobility, and cognitive engagement. Each influences the others. None operates in isolation for long.

The goal isn't some abstract idea of balance. It's alignment in how you actually live.

Sleep: The Anchor

Sleep anchors the system because it governs recovery, regulation, and repair.

Without adequate sleep, adaptation stalls. Strength gains flatten. Endurance erodes. Mobility stiffens. Cognitive engagement dulls. Decisions degrade.

Sleep is not a passive state. It is active maintenance. It restores physiological systems, consolidates memory, regulates hormones, and clears metabolic waste from the brain. It determines whether stress strengthens the system or overwhelms it.

In the long game, sleep is treated as infrastructure rather than a variable. It is protected not because it feels virtuous, but because it makes every other element work better.

When sleep is compromised, the system compensates briefly and then begins to fail.

Strength: Preserving Capability

Strength preserves the ability to exert force and maintain structure.

It protects bone density, joint integrity, and metabolic health. It supports posture and movement. It allows the body to resist decline rather than accommodate it.

Within The Longevity Playbook, strength is not about maximal output. It is about preserving capability across time. Training emphasizes consistency, control, and progressive exposure rather than peaks.

Strength supports endurance by improving efficiency. It supports mobility by stabilizing joints. It supports cognition indirectly by preserving confidence in movement and independence.

Strength is the body's refusal to become fragile.

Endurance: Sustaining Energy

Endurance determines how long capacity can be expressed without degradation.

It supports cardiovascular health, metabolic flexibility, and recovery. It expands the size of the energy reservoir rather than simply drawing from it.

In this system, endurance is not trained to exhaustion. It is trained to expand margin. A wide aerobic base allows stress to be absorbed without collapse. It shortens recovery time and reduces baseline fatigue.

Endurance improves sleep quality. It supports cognitive clarity. It allows daily life to feel less costly.

Without endurance, the system becomes brittle. Effort feels heavier. Participation narrows.

Mobility: Preserving Range

Mobility preserves the ability to move through space without friction.

It is the expression of usable range under control. Mobility allows strength and endurance to be applied without compensation. It keeps joints adaptable and movement fluid.

As people age, mobility often declines first and is addressed last. This inversion produces pain, restriction, and unnecessary limitation. The Longevity Playbook corrects this by treating mobility as maintenance rather than therapy.

Mobility supports sleep by reducing discomfort. It supports cognition by reducing chronic low-grade pain. It allows the body to remain cooperative rather than adversarial.

Cognitive Engagement: Sustaining the Mind

Cognitive engagement is the least visible component and one of the most important.

It reflects sustained curiosity, learning, reflection, and purpose. Cognitive engagement keeps the mind active, flexible, and adaptive. It prevents stagnation long before decline becomes clinical.

In this framework, cognition is not separated from the body. Physical vitality supports mental clarity. Mental clarity improves decisions around training, recovery, and life design. The loop closes.

Without engagement, longevity becomes hollow. Years accumulate, but meaning contracts.

The Reinforcing System

What distinguishes The Longevity Playbook from a routine is that its elements amplify one another.

Strength improves endurance. Endurance improves recovery. Recovery deepens sleep. Sleep sharpens cognition. Clear thinking improves decisions about movement, training, and life.

The system becomes lighter rather than heavier.

When aligned, these elements reduce the need for constant optimization. Decisions simplify. Effort feels proportional. The system sustains itself with less friction.

This is the opposite of burnout-driven health behavior. It is stewardship.

Capacity Across the Life Arc

Early in life, the playbook prevents erosion before it begins.

Habits established early compound. Capacity is accumulated rather than recovered. The system becomes resilient before stress accumulates.

Later in life, the playbook becomes restorative.

Strength can be rebuilt. Endurance can expand. Mobility can return. Sleep can improve. Cognitive engagement can deepen. The goal is not to reclaim youth, but to restore capability.

The body responds to intention at any age. What changes is tolerance for incoherence. This framework exists to preserve coherence.

Common Failure Modes

One failure is treating these elements as interchangeable. They are not. Improving one does not compensate indefinitely for neglecting another.

Another failure is prioritizing intensity over alignment. More effort applied to a misaligned system accelerates breakdown.

Some people over-focus on physical components while neglecting cognitive engagement. Others intellectualize longevity while allowing physical capacity to erode. Both lead to narrowing.

There is also the failure of rigidity. When the system becomes inflexible, it breaks under stress. The playbook requires adaptation, not perfection.

Applying the Model

This framework is not a set of instructions. It is a way to understand what is happening.

When energy begins to slip, look first at sleep and endurance. When pain starts to surface, revisit mobility and strength. When motivation feels flat, consider whether your mind is being engaged. The body and brain usually make the imbalance visible, if you are willing to pay attention.

Return to this playbook when your health starts to feel reactive or scattered. Use it to recalibrate, not to tear everything down and start over.

Over the years, this approach protects something more valuable than any single metric. It protects your ability to participate. It allows you to stay fully engaged in the life you are building, rather than slowly stepping back from it.

Longevity rarely happens by accident. It is shaped through alignment instead of rigidity, and through stewardship instead of constant optimization.

CLOSING REFLECTION: HOW TO USE THESE FRAMEWORKS

The frameworks in this Appendix are intentionally simple.

They are not simple because the subjects they address are simple. Health, wealth, judgment, time, and identity are not. They are simple because complexity rarely survives long horizons. Over decades, complexity obscures more than it reveals. What endures is structure.

Each framework here is a reduction. It strips away novelty, tactics, and short-term incentives to expose a few relationships that remain stable across time. They are not meant to impress. They are meant to orient.

If you are looking for precision, these frameworks may feel incomplete. They are not exhaustive. They are not optimized. They do not attempt to map every variable. That restraint is deliberate. A framework that tries to explain everything usually explains nothing for very long.

What matters in the long game is not total coverage. It is directional clarity.

Frameworks in Context

Many of these frameworks appear, in abbreviated form, throughout the main body of the book. That is intentional.

The narrative introduces them where ideas are best absorbed, in motion, alongside experience, reflection, and story. The Appendix gathers them in full, where they can be examined more closely, compared, and returned to repeatedly.

If certain models feel familiar, it is not repetition. It is reinforcement. Systems are learned through exposure, not explanation. The purpose of the Appendix is not novelty, but durability.

Frameworks as Systems, Not Advice

It is tempting to read frameworks as prescriptions. To ask what to do next. To look for steps, targets, or thresholds. That impulse is understandable, but it misses their purpose.

These frameworks are systems, not instructions.

A system describes how parts interact. It reveals leverage points. It makes tradeoffs visible. It allows you to anticipate second-order effects rather than reacting to first-order outcomes.

Advice expires quickly. Systems age slowly.

This is why the same frameworks can remain useful as circumstances change. The details of your life will evolve. Your career, family, resources, and constraints will not remain fixed. The relationships between effort and outcome, however, remain surprisingly consistent.

Compounding momentum still outperforms reset cycles. Capacity still widens opportunity. Structure still outperforms improvisation. Judgment still improves with continuity rather than volume.

The frameworks do not tell you what to choose. They help you see what choosing implies.

Mental Models That Compound

A useful mental model does more than explain the world. It shapes behavior without constant effort.

With time, these frameworks are meant to move from something you consult to something you carry. You do not need to actively recall them for them to work. When internalized, they change how situations are perceived before decisions are made.

You begin to notice imbalance earlier. You recognize drift before it becomes costly. You feel when complexity is increasing without corresponding benefit.

This is the power of good models. They reduce the need for vigilance by improving perception.

Most mistakes are not the result of ignorance. They are the result of delayed recognition. By the time a problem is obvious, compounding has already worked against you.

Frameworks shorten that delay.

Individually Useful, Collectively Stronger

Each framework in this Appendix stands on its own. You can return to one without consulting the others. That is intentional.

At the same time, their real strength emerges in combination.

The Tier 1 Civilian Protocol reinforces VO_2 max. VO_2 max reinforces the Quiet Arbitrage between Health and Wealth. Compounding Momentum explains why both succeed or fail in practice. The Thinking Loop shapes the judgment required to apply any of them consistently.

The Two Halves of Wealth explain why accumulation and preservation demand different instincts. Portfolio architecture translates those instincts into structure. Income sequencing extends them across time. Stewardship consolidates them into coherence.

This is not coincidence. It reflects how systems behave in the real world. No domain compounds in isolation for long. Health affects judgment. Judgment affects capital. Capital affects optionality. Optionality feeds back into how health and time are treated.

The frameworks are separate so they can be examined clearly. They are interdependent because life is.

Why Simplicity Matters More Over Time

Many people equate sophistication with effectiveness. In the short term, that can be true. In the long term, sophistication often becomes fragile.

Complex systems require constant attention. They demand maintenance. They create more failure points. They consume the very resources they were meant to enhance.

The frameworks in this Appendix are designed to resist that outcome.

They rely on first principles rather than optimization. They favor robustness over precision. They assume that life will interrupt plans, that motivation will fluctuate, and that attention will sometimes drift.

Simplicity survives those conditions. Complexity rarely does.

This is why the long game favors systems that continue working even when effort is imperfect. Not because imperfection is ideal, but because it is inevitable.

Using the Frameworks in Practice

You do not need to revisit these pages often. In fact, if you are reading them constantly, something is likely off.

The best time to return to a framework is when friction appears.

When progress stalls despite effort.

When decisions feel urgent rather than clear.

When complexity increases without corresponding benefit.

When fatigue accumulates quietly.

When optionality narrows unexpectedly.

These are system signals.

The frameworks are designed to help you diagnose rather than react. To identify which lever matters before pulling harder on all of them.

Often, the correction is smaller than expected. A shift in sequencing. A restoration of continuity. A simplification rather than an addition.

With consistency, this approach reduces the need for resets. Life becomes less episodic and more cumulative.

What These Frameworks Are Not

They are not guarantees.

They do not eliminate risk, uncertainty, or loss. They do not promise linear progress. They do not insulate you from randomness.

What they offer instead is durability.

They increase the probability that effort compounds rather than dissipates. They reduce the likelihood that success undermines itself. They help preserve the conditions under which a good life remains possible.

They also do not replace judgment. They depend on it.

A framework cannot tell you when to rest or push, simplify or expand, preserve or pursue. Those decisions remain contextual. What a framework can do is make the consequences of those decisions more visible.

It narrows the gap between intention and outcome.

Designed to Be Revisited

This Appendix is not meant to be read once and set aside permanently.

It is meant to age with you.

Some frameworks will feel more relevant in certain seasons. Others will recede temporarily. That is expected. The long game is not static. It unfolds in phases, even if it resists being lived in them.

What matters is that the reference remains available. That

when something feels off, there is a place to return that is not reactive, performative, or trend-driven.

A good framework does not demand attention. It waits.

The Long View

Most people dramatically underestimate the effect of compounding over long horizons. They focus on outcomes that are visible within months or years and ignore those that emerge slowly over decades.

The frameworks in this Appendix are built for those longer arcs.

They favor habits that do not feel heroic. Structures that do not attract attention. Decisions that appear conservative in the moment and obvious in retrospect.

They are designed for a life that is not optimized for applause, but for endurance.

That orientation is increasingly rare. It is also increasingly valuable.

Final Thought

If there is a single idea that unites these frameworks, it is this:

A well-designed life does not require constant intervention.

When systems are aligned, behavior becomes lighter. Decisions simplify. Effort compounds. Progress feels quieter but more reliable.

These frameworks are not meant to be followed rigidly. They are meant to be returned to periodically, adjusted thoughtfully, and carried forward with restraint.

Used well, they become less visible. They recede into the background. That is not a failure of the frameworks. It is their success.

They are there to support the long game.

ACKNOWLEDGEMENTS

A book like this is never created alone. It is shaped quietly over decades by the people who influence your thinking, challenge your assumptions, steady your direction, and remind you of what matters.

I want to thank the people who have traveled beside me in different seasons of life. Colleagues who sharpened my judgment. Mentors who taught me to think independently. Family and friends who created the conversations that became turning points. And teammates and coaches who showed me what disciplined work looks like, and how much clarity matters in complex environments. Their impact is in these pages even when their names are not.

To the writers and thinkers whose work has expanded my perspective: Charlie Munger, Warren Buffett, Gautam Baid, William Green, J. L. Collins, David Sinclair, and so many others. Their ideas reinforced my belief that curiosity compounds, that simplicity endures, and that the best answers are often the quietest ones. This book stands on ground they helped clear.

I'm grateful to the editors and creative partners whose insight and discipline strengthened the manuscript, and for the tools that supported research and revision along the way. Their contribution improved the work; any shortcomings remain my own.

And finally, to the readers. Whether you are twenty and building your foundation or fifty and beginning your next chapter, thank you for taking these ideas seriously. My hope is that this book offers something useful for the decades ahead. Something steady. Something durable. Something that lasts.

The long game is not just my philosophy. It is an evolving conversation. And I am grateful you are part of it.

ENDNOTES

1. Roy F. Baumeister et al., "Ego Depletion: Is the Active Self a Limited Resource?" *Journal of Personality and Social Psychology* 74, no. 5 (1998): 1252–1265.

2. B. J. Fogg, "A Behavior Model for Persuasive Design," in *Proceedings of the 4th International Conference on Persuasive Technology* (New York: ACM, 2009), 1–7.

3. Cal Newport, *Deep Work* (New York: Grand Central Publishing, 2016).

4. Raymond A. Mar, Keith Oatley, and Maja Djikic, "Emotion and Narrative Fiction," *Cognition & Emotion* 22, no. 3 (2008): 407–429.

5. Alan Jacobs, *The Pleasures of Reading in an Age of Distraction* (New York: Oxford University Press, 2011), 25–32.

6. K. Mandsager et al., "Association of Cardiorespiratory Fitness with Long-Term Mortality Among Adults Undergoing Exercise Treadmill Testing," *JAMA* 320, no. 19 (2018): 2022–2031.

7. Viktor E. Frankl, *Man's Search for Meaning* (Boston: Beacon Press, 1959).

8. Matthew Walker, *Why We Sleep: Unlocking the Power of Sleep and Dreams* (New York: Scribner, 2017).

9. Stanislas Dehaene, *Reading in the Brain* (New York: Viking, 2009).

10. J. R. R. Tolkien, *The Fellowship of the Ring* (London: George Allen & Unwin, 1954).

INDEX

A

E

Environment 17, 19, 43, 71, 81, 85, 91, 93

Exposure 19, 27, 49, 51, 53, 73, 85, 213

F

Focus 3, 13, 51, 71, 73, 91, 109, 113

Fragility 27, 49, 50, 51, 59, 71, 83, 91, 93

Freedom 3, 71, 73, 83, 109, 123, 125, 131

    – optionality expanding freedom 71, 73, 123, 177, 187

    – autonomy as financial outcome 71, 131, 145, 163, 187

G

H

I

ABOUT THE AUTHOR

Daniel Griffing is a life sciences advisor with three decades of experience across global healthcare companies.

His career has spanned IPO-stage biotech leadership, acquisition-driven exits, and global product launches at scale. Across these environments, he developed a long-term perspective on how decisions compound and how easily progress erodes without discipline and clarity.

Today, he leads GS & Partners, advising biotech executives and investors on new product development, market entry, and commercial strategy at the intersection of science and capital.

He is also the author of *The Long Game*, a monthly newsletter exploring the compounding of intellect, capital, and vitality. Shaped by a career building across continents, capital stages, and complexity, his work reflects a belief that durable advantage is designed, not improvised.

He has worked across Europe and the United States, including several years based in Zurich, Switzerland.

www.ingramcontent.com/pod-product-compliance
Lightning Source LLC
Chambersburg PA
CBHW020721150726
48196CB00036B/890/J